A DANCING PEOPLE

by
SISTER ADELAIDE ORTEGEL

Published by

THE CENTER FOR CONTEMPORARY CELEBRATION

West Lafayette, Indiana

Illustrations, Photography and Graphic Design by Adelaide Ortegel, S.P.

Special Photography Credits:

Michael A. Brown, 36,109
Kent Schneider, 72
Cathy Campbell, S.P., 113
Lorrayne Hockman, 147
Pacific Lutheran Liturgical
    Dance Ensemble, 48,50,59

CONTENTS

INTRODUCTION 1

CHAPTER 1

IN THE BEGINNING .... 2 - 16

CHAPTER 2

MOVING TOWARD WHOLENESS .... 17 - 35

CHAPTER 3

DANCE – A JOURNEY INTO FAITH .... 36 - 48

CHAPTER 4

DESIGNING DANCE FOR LITURGY .... 49 - 61
by Kathy Iverson-Beckman

CHAPTER 5

MIME - A LANGUAGE OF THE HEART .... 62 - 80

CHAPTER 6

SPIRIT - BODIED LITURGY ....by Kent Schneider .... 81 - 105

CHAPTER 7

CREATIVE MOVEMENT FOR EVERYONE .... 106 - 117

CHAPTER 8

MOVING TOGETHER .... 118 - 135

CHAPTER 9

LET'S HAVE A WORKSHOP .... 136 - 143

RESOURCES IN MUSIC AND FILM .... 144 - 147

INDEX 148

INTRODUCTION

<u>A DANCING PEOPLE</u> is designed to spotlight dance as a vital art form and an authentic faith expression that is accessible to everyone. It is designed to give fresh impetus to the dance leader, choreographer and dancer who may be involved in creating religious dance expression.

This is a book of ideas for you to work with. How they develop will depend upon the ingenuity, imagination and vision you can add.

In beginning this book, I feel as if I am opening before you an amazing old trunk that has been around the world since the beginning of time. Searching inside, we find new things and old: brightly colored folk dances, richly embroidered traditions, clown hats and space suits; golden links with the past and future, things to try on for size — a marvelous array of contributions from history and from people dancing today. This collection is yours to use in whatever way you choose. Dance in your own home, with small groups, with classes, at camp, on weekend retreats, in special times of celebration.

Dance has the power to renew —to enliven —to draw a people together. DANCING PEOPLE are people who can shake off the failures and disappointments of life, feel the Spirit quicken within them, and face the future with hope.

There are many DANCING PEOPLE who have helped me complete this book. Their spirit, as well as their words and photographs, fill the pages. I especially want to thank Kathy Iverson-Beckman, L'Ana Hyams-Burton, Marylu Milano, Mary Carroll Schindler, Gayda Errett and Kent Schneider for their writing, advice and inspiration. I am deeply grateful to Marcel Marceau for the personal time of sharing which he gave me. I thank Dolores Layer for her gracious assistance with the manuscript, and the photographers, dancers and workshop participants who added the spice of life to it all!

As a society, we are not yet a DANCING PEOPLE. We have been conditioned to a more rigid style of moving in the world. Technological progress has cost us dearly in individual human expressiveness. Except for the few, art is regimented and imitative —a spectator sport. Mass-production has meant artistic conformity. Hero-images in TV and movies have emphasized the cold, hard character who moves quickly, draws a gun, but seldom dances. Religious worship has separated the emotions from Spirit. Solemnity has come to mean proper posture, not DANCE. We are very much like the paralytic lying on his mat, waiting for the Lord to say, "Arise, take up your bed and walk." Let's rise to the invitation —walk! run! DANCE!

Whether you have the supple body of the dancer who has spent many years in training, or are just beginning, YOU have a spirit that can dance and a possibility for whole-bodied movement. Each one of us can get below our own surfaces and find unsuspected treasures...the artist, the dancer, the creative personality lying dormant.

SHIVA, Lord of the Dance, dances the five-fold dance of Creation, Veiling, Preservation, Destruction and Release. His aureole of fire emanates from the lotus pedestal; the prostrate Asura, demon of ignorance, lies underfoot. The god carries in his upper right hand a drum representing sound as the first element in the unfolding of the universe, while the upper left bears a tongue of flame, the element of the world's final destruction. The gestures of his other hands suggest the eternal rhythmic balance of life and death. One foot, resting on the demon of ignorance, the other raised in a dancing pose is interpreted to denote the circulation of consciousness into and out of the state of ignorance. He performs his dance both at the centre of the universe and within the "burning-ground" of the individual heart. Shiva's dance is the synthesis of all life experience and an image of all-pervading energy.

(Shiva Dancing, Bronze, India.)

chapter 1

IN THE BEGINNING

there was dance ...

```
"And the earth was without form, and void.
And darkness was upon the face of the deep.
And the spirit of God moved upon the face of the waters.
And God said: 'Let the waters bring forth abundantly
          the MOVING creatures
                        that have life."
                                    Genesis
```

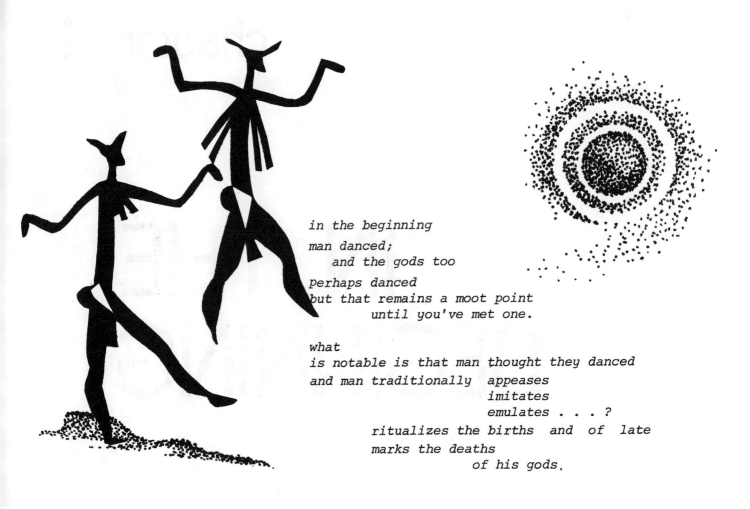

in the beginning

man danced;
    and the gods too

perhaps danced
but that remains a moot point
        until you've met one.

what
is notable is that man thought they danced
and man traditionally appeases
                        imitates
                        emulates . . . ?
            ritualizes the births and of late
            marks the deaths
                        of his gods.

The DANCE began with the first rhythmic steps of the first human persons walking this earth. As they absorbed the rhythms of the universe, the world of wind and waves and stars; the hopping, flying, swimming life a-round them, they felt the need to enter in...to be a part of these life movements.

   Listen to your own heartbeat. Feel the throb of your own pulse.
   Close your eyes and sense the rhythm of your own breathing.

Primitive people felt this exact same ebb and flow, pulsing of life. They tried to understand the meaning of it by responding to it with created rhythms of their own. Moving was ONE with thinking and feeling. Gesture was probably the first language. Each person began to search out a physical and emotional relationship with the world, as an individual and as a community. Feelings burst forth in song and dance.

Even now, it is with a hand clasp or a touch, that we speak the word we cannot say.

```
in the beginning
man danced, and
    (dancing)
     sounded sounds
     which were not the sounds
            of arrows
     which were not  the  sounds
            of hoes or wedges
     which were not the sounds
            of cookfires
               (when there were fires)
     but
were found sounds
discovered sounds
sought sounds

            man listened to  and
                 listened for
                          and
danced
        with remembering.
```

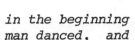

```
in the beginning
man danced.  and

        in his houses  (when he had houses)
            and holes  (before
                            he had houses)

        covered
           his walls with
what were not  skinpelts
                        with
what were not  greenleaves
but
   scratchings  and  colors
           which
were what he was   and
                was    becoming
                            and
let his eyes dance as well.
```

Dance became the vehicle or language for primitive man's religious expression.
He imitated the movement of life in nature. For him, movement indicated an
indwelling spirit. He searched for harmony with the world around him. Where
or when that harmony did not exist, he drew upon the power and energy of the
dance to change or appease the threatening forces. From the beginning, primitive man took his actual life experiences, times when the mystery of creation or suffering touched his life, and searched for the deeper meaning. With
the wholeness of mind and body, senses and emotions, he gave the meaning some
kind of <u>form</u> in ritualized gesture at the symbolic level.

5
```
```

```
in the beginning
man      not              beast wild or tame
         not fish
         nor bird of heaven  but
man,  danced.
and made music
   and
   arted his wonder
in
   recollection of the past,   a ritualization
in
   the grace of the present,   a revelry
in
   summoning of the future,   a hopeful vision
                              a prayerful supplication
            in
               celebration of his existence   which

                     bridges,
                     touches,
                     depends on,
                        gives meaning to all three
            and
            only man celebrates his existence

                  for only man is conscious of the
                           life-full
                     realities of his existence,
                           thank-full
                           hope-full

            for only man has, conscious of his existence
                        and
                           relative to his past
                     a
                        future to hope for
         and
         it is only in this hope-filled consciousness that
                                          man
                                          can
                                    celebrate
                                       "nevertheless"
               which is to say
         despite (and also because of) his now.
         man is celebrative
                  as he is  innovat-ive
                        recollect-ive
                              creat-ive
            and this makes him man

                     not chimp or porpoise.
```

We speak of primitive man as the ancestor of modern man, but also as actually present today. Primitive dances are still performed on South Pacific islands, in Africa, in Central and South America. Although many tribes have been exploited and changed by the white man's civilization, there are a few remote places where native dances have been preserved more or less intact. They can give us a fair idea of dances done several thousands of years ago.

Though the dance forms vary profusely from people to people and tribe to tribe, they all have the same function and mystery, to help man grasp his relationship to his God...or the controlling forces in the universe. To DANCE was/is total act of worship and prayer. The arts of mankind arose from these religious dances.

in the beginning
man danced.
which was - and incidentally is - to
c e l e b r a t e .
and this was magic
and
once again worship, which at the time
                    we could (in conscience)
                          equate.

 man still dances.   *(to be sure)*
 but his world is no more magic
                        but
            steel braced cities
                          rising mighty
                  a
     triumph of reasonableness
                practicality
                purposefulness
                utility
                a
      new myth of hereandnow power
                which can serve
          or   demand service
                          rendered
and when he dances   it is almost *sadness*

he must repent of his wonder
        to live his myths
        which are   not
          sung   myths
        which are   not
         danced   myths
        which are   not
          arted   myths   *(and hold him somber)*
              but

newsprint
     blueprint
          fineprint redink   timecard
                          punchcard
                          chargecard mysteries

       he's locked in (freely).

7

```
            forgetting the magic
            forgetting his dance
            forgetting even  to shout
                            to reach  to cry
                            to run  to hug  to wish
                            which  is  to  say
            forgetting the  c e l e b r a t i o n
                        which
              keeps his myths  and his soul  and his
                        world
            so hopefully human.

            if man  be man  he needs again  to learn
                                        to celebrate
            which is  to sing and dance
            and wondering,  laugh  which is fully human
                    which is worship as well.
```

Marylu Milano

Marylu Milano wrote the poem, "In the Beginning," as a way of expressing her convictions about the evolution of religion, celebration, and man's need to dance. This poem has been choreographed for dancers and visuals, accompanied by drums, bells, and electronic music. Marylu is a talented dancer who has combined her love for dance with an intense study of theology and Scripture. After graduating from Mundelein College in Chicago, Marylu received a Danforth Scholarship to continue her studies in dance and theology to the doctoral level. She has been a part of several multi-media celebrations enabled by The Center For Contemporary Celebration.

Beginnings of Western Civilization

In studying the styles of religious dance as civilization progressed, it is significant to note that the movements of the dance reflected the understanding the people had of the object worshipped. The worship of earth spirits called forth an imitation of elements in nature. For example, there is an abundance of material documenting the religious dances of the American Indians who worshipped the Great Spirit in all of nature. The Greeks, who developed a religion of anthropomorphic gods, created dance forms which expressed the nature of these gods. The dances emphasized dignity, beauty, grace. They had their roots in ritual, but they were not appeasing or supplicating dances. The dances manifested the relationship between the people and their gods. They stated the philosophy and myth of the people in a splendidly dramatic way.

The Greeks had a broad concept of dancing. It included victory processions, weapon dances and displays of power. The art of dance was a rhythmic ball game, a funeral or wedding procession, or the flowing movements of a trained chorus on stage. In their quest for beauty and perfection of movement, the Greeks appreciated dance as an aesthetic experience.

The Romans tried to transplant, by force, the majesty and delicacy of Greek dance to their own shores. They imported the dancing choruses from Greece and the other islands for their great spectacles. But, the Romans were incapable of understanding or appreciating the cultural background or the religious philosophy of the Greek art form. The spiritual quality and the art deteriorated. These two are inseparable. Dance became degraded, a source of entertainment indulged in more for sensual delight than for artistic expression. Movement, so clearly and truthfully reflects feeling that it has always been a mirror of the moral attitude of a people.

> *"Probably all art loses its deeper justification
> when divorced from religion."*
>
> *Walter Sorell*

Hebrew Religious Dance

In another part of the Mediterranean world, wandering tribes of Israelites received the knowledge of one Supreme Being, the Lord Yahweh. Their God made a covenant with them. He would be a Protector and a Strength for them.

Like primitive tribes, it was natural for the Hebrews to express states of joy or sadness, praise or supplication, in an out-pouring of dance and song. They danced for festivals, weddings, anniversaries and births with a spontaneous, unself-conscious freedom. They danced in their worship of Yahweh. They wrote Psalms (prayer songs) to be danced by the throngs of people approaching the Temple on the high holidays.

> *"Alleluia!*
> *Sing Yahweh a new song,*
> *let the congregation of the faithful sing his praise!*
> *Let Israel rejoice in his maker,*
> *and Zion's children exult in their King;*
> *let them dance in praise of his name,*
> *playing to him on strings and drums!"*
>
> *Psalm 149*

> *"Hear, O Lord, and have pity upon me,*
> *O Lord, be my helper: You have*
> *changed my mourning into dancing..."*
>
> *Psalm 30:11-13*

Unlike primitive religious dance, however, the Hebrew sacred dance took on a new, more personal character. The Israelites danced in praise and thanksgiving for the blessings of a loving, caring God. They did not dance in fear or in order to appease the gods. Nor did they design dances to dramatize their relationship with God. Their dances were an expression of religious emotion. They were a whole-hearted casting off of earthly ties, worries and sinful desires. Their dances exulted in the freedom and trust that they were God's Chosen People.

There were times when they slipped from this ideal. In the Book of Exodus we read of Moses condemning the Hebrews for dancing around the golden calf:

> *"I am grieved," he cried to Yahweh, "this people has committed a grave sin, making themselves a god of gold."*

The Israelites had fallen back into a kind of magic or propitiatory dance which was a turning away from their new covenant with Yahweh.

There is mention of individuals dancing for the Lord; such as Miriam, leading the women in a dance of thanksgiving after crossing the Red Sea safely. King David danced with all his might before the Lord, with something of the bravado of a Muhammad Ali. But, in general, the dance was a communal act of worship or celebration. There was hardly any clear-cut line between the ritual of the Temple and the festivals of the people. Biblical man danced as a natural expression of his beliefs, without being aware of the aesthetic feelings or rules to be found in more advanced cultures. The community, the extended family, growing in God's loving care, were the main concern. Dance expressed the collective well-being of the people.

Early Christian Liturgical Dance

As a small seed, Christianity began to grow and spread in lands that held the widely differing views of Greeks, Romans, Hebrews and all the other peoples of the Middle East. Some of the art and culture of each land was assimilated into the new religion. There is evidence to show that the early Christians used dance in their liturgies whenever it was their natural expression and a part of their religious tradition. In areas where dance had become decadent and connected with orgies, as in the city of Rome, it was shunned as pagan. In other parts of the early Christian world it was used in connection with the most sacred mysteries of the Church.

Eusebius, the father of Church History, quotes from a description of the worship of the Therapeuts by Philo:

> *After the banquet they keep the sacred all-night festival. And this is how they keep it. They all stand up in a body, and in the middle of the banqueting-place` they first form two choroi, one of men and the other of women, and a leader and conductor is chosen for each, the one whose reputation is greatest for a knowledge of music; then they chant hymns composed in God's honor in many metres and melodies, sometimes singing together, sometimes one choros beating the*

measure with their hands for the antiphonal
chanting of the other, now dancing to the
measure and now inspiring it, at times dancing in
procession, at times set-dances, and then circle-
dances right and left.

We also possess the Gnostic "Hymn of Jesus" from the Apocrypha Second-Century Acts of John. This wonderful hymn is the earliest Christian ritual of which we know. It is interpreted as a sacred dance wherein the newborn disciple is united with the Master; the purified human nature with the Divine Presence. It clearly describes the Last Supper, at which Christ takes leave of his disciples. It is the source of the Catholic Mass, which originally was a dance, a divine pantomime.

John tells us that Jesus gathered his disciples around him, before going out to fulfill the destiny of his passion and death. He invites them to move in a circle dance. In the unity of this sacred dance, he speaks to them:

Hymn from the Apocryphal Acts of John

(Selected)

Glory be to the Father.
And we, going about in a ring, answered him,
Glory be to thee, Word: Glory be to thee,
        O Grace,   AMEN.
I would be saved, and I would save.   AMEN.
Grace danceth. I would pipe; dance ye all.
I would mourn; lament ye all.   AMEN.
The whole world on high hath part in our dancing.   AMEN.
Who so danceth not, knoweth not what cometh
            to pass.
I would be united and I would unite.   AMEN.

The disciple must repeat the acts of the Lord if he is to become like him, to achieve union with him. This was symbolized by the answering of AMEN and a responsive movement in the dance. It had the form of a Holy Office or Litany that was chanted within the circle:

    A torch am I to thee that beholdest.   AMEN.
    A mirror am I to thee that perceivest me.   AMEN.
    A door am I to thee that knockest at me.   AMEN.
    A way am I to thee a wayfarer.   AMEN.

This sacred circle dance was followed by the AGAPE, the LOVE FEAST, and the custom of sharing the kiss of peace.

If it is difficult to conceive of Jesus leading a dance, perhaps we need to look more closely at some of the things Jesus said in the New Testament and try to understand them in the context of the Hebrew culture of that time.

11

We read that after Jesus had called the twelve apostles to be a part of his ministry, he gathered crowds of people around him and began to teach. This collection of his teachings has come to be known as the Sermon on the Mount. He said:

> *How happy are you who are poor: yours is the kingdom of*
> *God.*
> *Happy you who are hungry now: you shall be satisfied.*
> *Happy you who weep now; you shall laugh.*
> *Happy are you when people hate you, drive you out, abuse you, denounce*
> *your name as criminal, on account of the Son of Man. Rejoice when*
> *that day comes and dance for joy, then your reward will be great in*
> *heaven. This was the way their ancestors treated the prophets.*
>
> *Luke 6: 20-23*

In Aramaic, the language which Jesus spoke, the word for "rejoice" is the same as the word for "dance". The people would have understood the use of the word in this context as a literal invitation to dance. They would have identified with the idea of "dancing" as a means for regaining joy and hope, as well as a way of expressing it.

The Growth of Christianity

The Christians brought a new idea to the world of power structures. They believed that, before God, all men and women, rich and poor, slave or freeman, stand equal. Men, women and children are valuable and possess individual dignity. Sharing, eating together, dancing together, praying together, were all ways to express this commonality.

The Greeks believed that there was an after-life and danced a ring dance to mark the safe passage of the deceased. Early Christians drew upon this custom and circled the grave with a lively funeral dance to celebrate a person's birth into everlasting life. Rose petals were dropped on the open grave as they sang: "Ring around the rosie, a pocket full of posies, ashes, ashes, we all fall down."

The early Christians, despising Greek and Roman ritual, soon developed liturgies of their own. Nevertheless, they drew upon the beautiful customs and symbols of the older religions —bells, candles, incense, folk melodies and dancing. They were given new interpretations and woven into the celebrations of Christian mysteries. Dances in churches began to blossom. Sacred dances celebrated the anniversaries of martyrs' deaths. Such rites were performed in several ways: by one or many dancers as a "round" or procession, using a solo voice or instrument as accompaniment or combined with a singing choir.

From time to time the dance became too boisterous and out of hand. Church leaders were quick to suspect a return to pagan practices. Forcefully, dance and drama were moved outside of the church proper and performed on the church steps or at holiday fairs.

Dancing and Singing, or Just Singing?

The traditional Christmas Carols were a part of this interplay of folk art and religious worship. The true Carols were folk melodies of the people. Some were adapted from pagan festivals and given Christian words. A Carol was meant to be danced. The word itself comes from the Italian "Carolare," a medieval ring dance accompanied by singing. The Carols were so closely linked with dance that they, too, often suffered exclusion from the church proper. They became associated with the Miracle and Morality Plays which originated in the 8th Century.

The plays were given in churches, in the streets, and at fairs. They reflected one of the characteristic features of early Christian thought: otherworldliness. The emphasis was transferred from this world to the kingdom after death. Sharp distinctions were drawn between good and evil, mind and body, spirituality and carnality. The important thing was to save the soul. The body was considered a hindrance. Dance, because of its physical and pleasurable nature, was frowned upon and often suppressed. As time went on it was permitted to exist only in the very formal ritual gestures of the Mass and solemn processions.

Writing in the 5th Century, St. Augustine encouraged the people and the Church to understand the literal call "to dance" in a more symbolic or "spiritual" way. He was quoting from the Psalms 149 and 150:

> "Let them praise his name in chorus." (verse 3)
> What meaneth "chorus"? Many know what a "chorus"
> is; nay, as we are speaking in a town, almost all
> know. A "chorus" is the union of singers. If we
> sing "in chorus," let us sing in concord. The
> whole world is now the chorus of Christ. The
> chorus of Christ soundeth harmoniously from east
> to west.

(Augustine, "Exposition of Psalms," *The Nicene and Post Nicene Fathers*, first series, 8, New York, 1888, p. 678.)

The word "chorus" from the Latin "chorea" is a translation from the Hebrew of a word meaning "to dance in a circling group." Augustine's interpretation had shifted the meaning. The word "chorus" remained in the Psalms, but came to be understood as "to sing in a group."

Augustine was plagued with the tension between body and soul. He was writing in a chaotic time, trying to establish an understanding of the spiritual dimensions of human life, defending the Catholic Church against heretics. His writings greatly influenced the theological and philosophical thinking of the world for centuries to come.

Later, during the pontificate of Gregory the Great, dance was officially excluded from the Catholic liturgy. Music and drama went out with the dance, but music was allowed back under strict surveillance. The Church grew to be more and more authoritarian. The emphasis of the Christian social message became:

> "*Life means hardship to be endured in preparation for the life to come.*"

The early Christian spirit of gladness was clouded over and obscured by the spirit of guilt and fear.

The Eastern Orthodox liturgy has preserved the early Christian mood of rejoicing in the gift of salvation. The Eucharistic meal is shared in the exultant celebration of the Resurrection, rather than in the recollection of the death of Christ. Processions and spontaneous gestures are still very much a part of the Eastern Church liturgy. There are no chairs or pews in their churches. The people stand through the whole service, thus, movement can take place naturally, without the hindrance of furniture.

In the Western Church, religious dramas and festivals continued, but outside of the church building. During the Renaissance, dance returned to the sanctuary for a brief time. Music and art flourished in richly festive array. Then came the final blow. With the invention of the printing press and the distribution of books, a growing emphasis was placed upon the intellect, at the expense of the body and the emotions. Our worship services are still laboring under this handicap. Next, came the Reformation, which again swept away most of the arts, leaving only the printed and preached word, and a limited amount of music. The Counter Reformation in the Catholic Church did much the same thing. Dance, from this point on, became established as secular entertainment. It was thought of as something frivolous and profane...a pastime for the idle rich or a diversion for the lower classes in the streets.

Some branches of Protestant Christianity, the Calvinists, including most New England Puritans, went so far as to teach that all dancing of any kind, anywhere, was sinful and a direct trap of the devil. Church music was written to avoid the kind of rhythms that would encourage toe-tapping.

Dancing, for Western man, was cut off from its roots and natural inspiration. The communal dancing survived in the folk dances of the people. These same dances were polished by the nobility in their luxurious ballrooms and became courtly entertainment. Presentations by groups of highly stylized dancers evolved into the form known as "ballet."

A Secularized Culture

The rise of capitalism, industrialism and scientific discovery continued forcing the ever-widening gulf between the sacred and the secular. The newly emerging middle class became interested in the enjoyment of this life. Art became separated from religious symbolism and content. It became the creation of the individual rather than the group. This individualism led to technical experimentation and personal artfulness in solo dance styles. Ballet became professional and went over to the theater.

Dance in America Today

Dance is an expression of the age that produces it. It reveals the spirit of its own times. All the complex diversities of the social and political forces of history have shaped our attitudes toward dance today. In America there is a growing consciousness and understanding of dance by a wider range of people. Television is constantly improving its presentation of dance sequences. The major dance companies are offering an exciting variety of styles and experiences. Almost every large college campus has an experimental dance group. Sessions in modern dance and creative movement are held in schools and clubs around the country.

Modern dance and jazz are the two great art-forms created by Americans. Both have gained world-wide recognition. Both depend upon expressive communication and improvisation, combined with complete mastery of the instrument.

The history of modern dance, beginning with Isadora Duncan and her revolt against the artificiality and restrictions of classical ballet, is a fascinating account. In this brief overview I can highlight only a few of the outstanding dance innovators who reversed the direction of dance, restoring it to its rightful position as an art of deep spiritual expressiveness.

Ruth St. Denis was a beautiful dancer with a radiant personality who introduced oriental dancing to the American stage. She not only delighted the eyes of the viewers with her exotic costumes and settings, but also shared something of the mystic religious connotation. She became a crusader for the sacred dance. In the Twenties, she met and married Ted Shawn, who shared her belief in the essential religious quality of true dance. Together, they founded the Denishawn school and dance company. Technically this was the beginning of modern dance in America and the training ground for a new generation of dance leaders. But, more than that, a spiritual revolution was begun. Young dancers from the Denishawn school wanted to explore the spiritual dimensions of their own times... to dance out the things that concerned them.

Foremost of the Denishawn students was Martha Graham, a magnificent dancer and the most unique and prolific dance creator America has known so far. She invented entirely new styles and techniques of moving. Beyond that, she developed dance as a dramatic language of inner emotion. Her stage settings were stripped to the barest essentials. In her many portraits of mythological and Biblical heroines, she probed deeply into the human psyche. She wanted to free the American spirit from the bonds of Puritanism and industrial enslavement.

It is this return to the fundamental sources of dance expression that has inspired the growing interest in revitalizing sacred dance. Small groups of people all over this country and Canada are dedicating immense energy and love to the task of creating and nurturing religious dance.

There is something about dance that constantly renews itself and those involved in it. It is a living art that draws from the pulsing life-principle within each of us.

FURTHER READING

DeMille, Agnes. The Book of Dance. Paul Hamlyn Ltd., London, 1963.
   A richly illustrated historical and artistic development of dance.

Duncan, Isadora. Art of the Dance. Theatre Arts, New York, 1928.
   Important for understanding Isadora Duncan's contribution to modern dance.

Fraser, Sir John. The Golden Bough. Macmillan Co., New York, 1947.
   Traces the roots of dance and celebration in myth and legend and in the
   folk traditions and customs.

Gopal, Ram. Indian Dancing. Phoenix House, London, 1951.

Haskell, Arnold L. The Wonderful World of Dance. Garden City Books, Garden
   City, New York, 1960.
   Very fine historical background.

Letherman, Leroy. Martha Graham: Portrait of the Lady as an Artist. Knopf,
   New York, 1966.
   Gives an insight into the creative intuition of an outstanding woman.

St. Denis, Ruth. My Unfinished Life. Harper, New York, 1939.

Shawn, Ted. Every Little Movement. Ted Shawn, New York, 1954.

Sorell, Walter. The Dance through the Ages. Grosset & Dunlap, New York, 1967.
   Sorell traces the history of the dance from primitive rites and tribal
   dances to the dancers of today who are exploring the frontiers of the art.

Terry, Walter. The Dance in America. Harper & Row, New York, 1956.

chapter 2

*"I believe that dance is the oldest, noblest
    and most cogent of the arts.
I believe that dance is the most perfect
    symbol of the activity of God and His angels.
I believe that dance has the power to heal,
    mentally and physically.
I believe that true education in the art of
    dance is education of the whole man..."*

                              from Ted Shawn's Creed

moving toward
WHOLENESS

The first chapter deals with the story of dance, as we know it
from history. It is a story of creative actions and reactions,
beginnings and adaptations.   This chapter deals with a closer
look at the basic element and source of all dance, that is,
MOVEMENT.   Modern dance evolved as a response to a vital need
to break with traditional forms of classical dance movement,
in order to find freer and more personal kinds of movement
expression. The language and experience of expressive movement is open to anyone who will take the time to look within,
                                            with feeling.

Our Own Experience of Movement

Movement is so natural to us that we often are completely unaware of it.
Our whole life process consists of FEELING
                                          SENSING
                                                THINKING
                                                      MOVING.
When one of these elements is missing, the whole process disintegrates.

SENSORY AWARENESS

Try sitting motionless for even sixty seconds.

It soon becomes uncomfortable. You probably begin thinking, "Why am I
doing this? How dumb this feels." You'll notice that your eyelids blink.
The feeling of suffocation will make you inhale, causing movement in the
chest and diaphragm. Your muscles begin to feel tense and unnatural.
By trying to remain motionless for a brief time, you become much more a-
ware of what it means to be able to move. Without movement, life cannot
continue.

Our senses are channels of communication with the world outside of our
bodies. It is through the senses that we bring the outer world into our
inner world. Without some form of sense-ability, there is no life. When
one of the senses is limited or ignored, then the whole process is limited.
When one of the senses dominates, there is a lack of harmony. Life is a
little lop-sided. It is not whole.

Our one-sidedness tends to be in a mind-dominated style of existence. We
live too much of the time simply within our heads, depending upon our eyes
and the written word or visual image. We read or view television or listen
to music as a second-hand experience. We have deprived ourselves of the
first-hand experiencing that involves the whole life process of using all
of our senses, our feelings, our ability to think and move independently
and creatively.

For the last few years, we have heard and read a great deal about the importance of sharpening our sensitivity or "heightening our awareness."
Quite often brave beginnings are made and then people aren't sure what to
do with their newly awakened senses. There needs to be an opportunity for
continued growth.

There is much study and experimentation going on in different parts of the
world in pursuit of more wholistic styles of life for contemporary persons.
Dr. Moshe Feldenkrais, working in Tel Aviv, has developed a philosophy and
some techniques for building better body habits and invoking new dimensions
in awareness, self-image and human potential. In his book, AWARENESS
THROUGH MOVEMENT, he explains his theories and methods in practical, easy-
to-use exercises that help you grow in sensory awareness.

There are centers in our own country where workshops and sessions in body awareness and creative movement are being offered regularly. Men and women in contemporary society are beginning to recognize the need to get back in touch with their bodies. We have been cut-off from free and natural movement by the dictates of civilized behavior. Human progress has meant overcoming animal instincts. Many aggressive tendencies in human behavior can be traced back to earlier stages in the developmental process. Territorial possession, loyalty to the herd, hostility to members of any other herd, struggles for position and dominance; all seem to be rooted in our instincts.

One way to deal with the passions has been to suppress them. Clamp down on all display of emotion in order to gain control. This is negative, repressive action. AWARENESS offers another alternative. The truly creative people, the peace-MAKERS of the world, have been and are, persons who have integrated their ability to FEEL SENSE THINK OUT MOVE into action. In other words, they have developed the art of AWARENESS. They have gained the SENSE-ability to pause between outward stimuli and reflex or immediate action, and in that space, understand wider dimensions and relationships. AWARENESS is far different from suppression or self-control. It is an opening and channeling of the whole life process toward positive, creative growth.

AWARENESS means being fully alive to an experience at a fully human level. It means thinking which is in touch with deeper sensings and feelings. AWARENESS has all the brand new freshness of spring blossoms, the miracle of rebirth.

Is it possible to open the way for AWARENESS, or is it a gift?
Can it be taught? or only caught?
Is it a melting process, like an early spring thaw?
Or, is it a planting process that must wait for the ground to be readied?

How Does AWARENESS Happen?

From the experiences that I have had with students and workshop groups of every type, I would say that it happens in a limitless number of ways, like spring itself, and it can be developed or nurtured by anyone who will take the time to seek it.

A Workshop Experience:

A white-haired, sixty-one year old minister registered for one of our workshops. It was a week-long intensive in the arts of celebration. The minister arrived late, missing the opening ideas. People were in the midst of creating some non-verbal expressions of what they believed about God, the world and themselves. He moved on the fringes of the activity, a somewhat critical observer. He listened to the sharings, contributing nothing, but trying to understand how colors, textures, shapes and found items could possibly express the ideas people were talking about.

"I just don't see it," he said.
"These colors and uneven shapes don't say anything to me."
"How can scraps of color represent people?"
"But that's what I'm here for ——to try to learn about this kind of thing."

The next morning we began with creative movement. We worked as individuals and in groups; exploring space, levels of energy, heaviness and lightness, machine movements. Then we began to work in small groups, designing dance statements to share with each other. It was a "first" for him and for just about everyone else in the group. He was surprised at how free it felt and how expressive it could be. Slowly his defensive, critical attitude began to soften and change. During a session on photography he was able to help others. This was his special art. He was able to resume his role as leader, but in a different way. By the third day he was making a fine non-verbal banner with bright colors, wild textures and (significantly) two dancing figures in the vista of creation. By the fourth day he chose to be a part of the creative dance group which shared a prayer expression on stage for a large group of people.

If he had walked on water, the transformation could not have been more amazing. The hostility which we had sensed in the man had been very real. Beyond photography he had never really risked himself to express his feelings. We learned later that people who knew him had been holding their breath in regard to his participation.

The change in this particular man was somehow linked with the risk he took to get in touch with deeper sensings within himself. It was the freeing experience of the creative movement that opened a new kind of awareness for him personally. The freedom and sensitivity carried over into the other arts and into the ability to receive the creative offerings of others in a new way.

What is the connection between AWARENESS and religious expression?
What is the theological dimension of creativity and the arts?
Do the creative arts really have a rightful place in communal worship?

These are important questions that come up over and over again. The answers seem obvious, yet difficult to put in words. Awareness, Creative Expression and God's Creating Love are a circle of inter-related energies. One leads naturally into the others if the channels are open.

> AWARENESS is that crystalline moment when we are able to feel
> and comprehend more clearly, more wholly.

> CREATIVE EXPRESSION is the vehicle for the natural out-flowing
> of awareness and intuition.

> GOD'S CREATING LOVE is the power of God to touch us now,
> individually and collectively.

It is in the coming-together of these three energies that I see dynamic possibilities for growth within the individual and within the community which we call Church. It is vitally important that we understand this convergence and interplay, especially if we are in the ministry of dance or any of the other creative arts.

Unfortunately, many people have a misconception of the role of the arts in worship. The place of music is usually held in esteem with certain limits as to style and mode. The visual arts and dance are often thought of as ornamentation, novelties, for the children, etc. In all truth, the arts, with the fullness of creative inspiration, are at the very heart of religious expression.

Human nature is made in the image and likeness of God. Creativeness is the quality that most clearly shows this family resemblance. Creative inspiration is the moving of God within the depths of our being. It is a unique religious experience in itself.

Before dance and the other arts can be truly at home in the Church and able to proclaim their joy, there is need for a realization of the authentic religious nature of their communication. Before we can be a "Dancing People," we must learn to value and trust our own creative sensings. If the Church is to be a living force in the world today, it is crucial that this kind of spiritual sensitivity and creative consciousness be affirmed.

> THE ARTIST, in a sense, is able to help us see in new ways. He
> helps us to wonder with the mystery and the beauty of it all.
> He presents surprises which open another facet of creation to us.

> The GROWTH OF AWARENESS opens us to receive the creating of the
> artist and the creating love of God.
> It liberates us from the conformity and uniformity of so
> much of modern life. It frees us from our own compulsions

and the restrictions that we feel pressing upon us. It
frees us for creating, which means that we, too, can be
peace-MAKERS and love-MAKERS.

GOD'S CREATING LOVE is the ground from which all this grows;
        the energizing source and final meaning. His love gives
        purpose to the creating and to the awareness.

Christ as Artist

Christ himself was an artist, helping us to see beneath the surface.
His stories penetrated the ordinary things of everyday life in order to
discover the unique and the personal. Common things, like the lost coin,
the mustard seed, the birds of the field, the widow's mite, revealed an
inner truth. He taught in parables, poetic images from life experiences.
He did not explain everything in minute detail or in "one...two...three
things to remember" order. He trusted us to live out the right response
and action in our own lives. He awakened the imagination and allowed the
understanding to grow individually within each person.

>   *"But to what shall I compare this generation?*
>   *It is like children sitting in the market places*
>   *and calling to their playmates,*
>
>   *'We played the pipes for you,*
>   *and you wouldn't dance.*
>   *We sang dirges,*
>   *and you wouldn't be mourners.'"*   Matt. 11:16-17

Jesus criticizes the people who are not moved by a message of joy or a
message of sorrow. They will not listen to John the Baptist or to Jesus.
The invitation, the challenge, leaves them apathetic. Jesus is saying:

>   *"You are not acting naturally, wholly.*
>   *You are not responding as fully human persons."*

He would stir them and us to a greater AWARENESS:

   Happy the gentle... *those who sense the weakness and*
                           the needs of others.

   Happy those who mourn... *those who have cared enough to cry,*
                               who have shared love.

   Happy those who hunger and thirst for justice... *those who*
                           sense the injustices shown to others
                           as if they were their own.

Happy the merciful... *those who can feel the pain of another,*
those who can feel a oneness with suffering.

Happy the pure in heart... *those who are not wearing masks or*
playing games with the feelings of others.

Happy the peace-MAKERS... *those who can search out alternatives*
and build for the future.

Happy those who can DANCE... *when they are persecuted for*
my name's sake.

Jesus came to bring us the WHOLENESS of life, from our innermost souls to
the very tips of our fingers and the tapping of our toes.

There is a definite place and a crying need for creative imagination, for
music, metaphor and dance in the Church today. It is important for each
individual member and for the community as a living witness to the creating
presence of God. Liturgical celebrations should be expressions of whole
living. They should be hopeful visions of possibilities that go beyond the
disjointed, fragmentary happenings of daily life. The liturgy should help
life make sense.

Dance is the art expression that is distinctively and by its very essence
capable of communicating WHOLENESS. It is a celebration of being, and of
being-in-tune-with the roots of existence.

Laura Callahan reminds us that, when you are three years old, life is
for living and to dance is as natural as breathing.

DANCE as an Art to Be Experienced

Keeping in mind all that has been said about the power of creativity and the importance of awareness, let's try to get a better understanding of DANCE as an expressive art.

Since DANCE involves no other tool than the body, and not just a part, but the whole body, it is a vehicle for expressing wholeness or the search for wholeness. You might say, the medium (the body) is the message.

We are not spirit imprisoned in a body. We are spirit and body...a total being. We are limited by our bodies, but we are also challenged by them. A person cannot live by intellect alone.

We have been conditioned to distrust the body with its senses and emotions. Our scientific age idolizes "fact." Our educational system is built on the process of delivering massive amounts of "fact." The intuitive, the creative, cannot be tested and systematized, so it is given a small backroom or it is put into books for us to read about in the second-hand experience of the printed word.

The art of DANCE, the experience of DANCE, is something you can't possibly know by reading about it. It cannot be mass produced, that is, put in a kit and sent to you to be put together or played. It has to be re-created each time. Even film or videotape cannot capture the actual spirit of it. At best, it can give you only a partial idea of the whole. Unless you experience being caught up in its rhythms, or can free yourself to explore it as a communicative way of moving, you can't really know Dance.

Movement Explorations

On the next pages are some MOVEMENT EXPRESSIONS in the form of simple exercises. You can try them by yourself or with a group. Make them your own. Adapt them any way you wish, but don't just read about them. Try them.

The CENTERING exercise is especially important as a way to begin every creative movement experience. First of all, it tunes one in to an inner awareness of life and movement. Secondly, it helps to relax muscles and nerves. It can have endless variations, but it should have the elements of helping you get in touch with your body and the space around you, and giving your body the freedom to move naturally and in new ways.

CENTERING has some characteristics of YOGA EXERCISES and MEDITATION, but it allows for more individuality and personal creating. I have included the COSMIC BREATHING exercise of YOGA. Breathing in the new, the fresh, and the good, or breathing out the stale, the tensions and the divisiveness, are also a part of CENTERING in preparation for MOVEMENT or PRAYER.

25

CENTERING

Read the entire exercise first. Recall or re-read the main actions,
then take your time in trying them out. Take about 10 or 15 minutes.

In order to loosen up and relax, take off your shoes.

BECOMING AT HOME IN THE SPACE

Stand in some open space in the room.
Plant your feet squarely on the floor, a little bit
apart. Close your eyes. Without moving your feet
see how far you can reach in every direction. Explore
that total circumference of air around you.

Breathe slowly and deeply as you sculpt the space
around you. For the present, this is your space.

CENTERING THE BODY & MIND

Now sit down in this space. Feel the floor around you.
Try to find the center, your own center, within this space.
Sit with legs crossed or in some way that is comfortable
for you and will allow you to be poised in a balanced
position.

If your neck and shoulders feel tense, gently roll your
head around, first in one direction, then in the other.
Collapse your shoulders and chest, and then come back to
a balanced position where it is easy to take deep breaths.
There should be a bouyancy rather than a stiff, straight-
ness about you. If your legs feel tight or cramped, slap
them gently from thighs to ankles. Find a comfortable
position and come back to center.

BUILDING A RHYTHM

Listen intently to any sounds which may be around you or
within you. Build a rhythm pattern with hands tapping
the floor or knees. Let the rhythm grow until it feels
like a natural part of you. Tap it with the whole palm
of your hand on the floor. Let the rhythm fade slowly,
and once again bring your body back to a centered position.

CLOSING AND OPENING

Bring your knees up to your body and grasp them with your
arms. Wrap yourself up as tightly as you can. Become
impenetrable...like a rock. Hold this tension for a few
seconds. Be aware of the strain and contraction of muscles
in your back and arms.

Very slowly begin to release this tension of muscles. Let
your whole frame gently open as if it were melting. Not
just your arms, but your entire body. Feel as if the
water is now surrounding you and supporting you.

Very quickly contract all your muscles again and become
closed...rock-like. Begin the very slow release and
opening movement.

CENTERING

Return to the CENTERED position. Remain quiet for a few moments
before beginning the next experience.

Cosmic Breathing

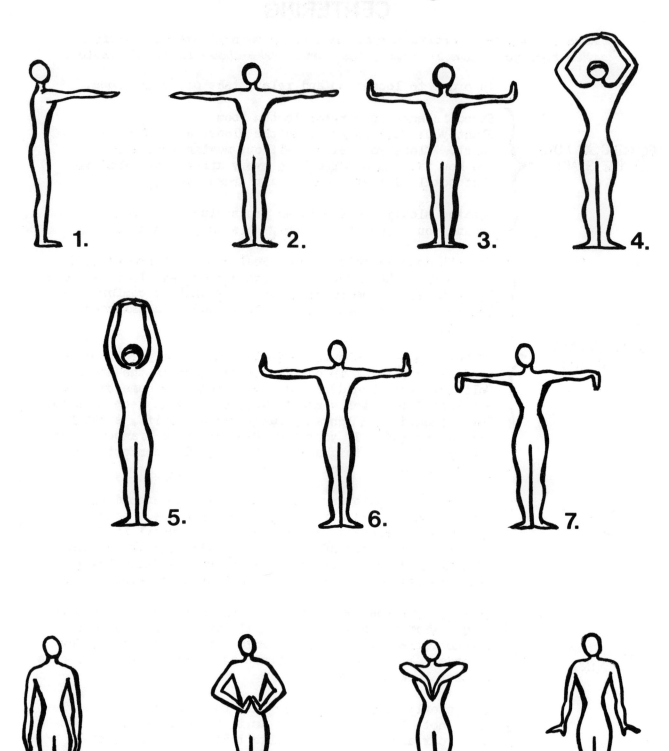

COSMIC BREATHING

In YOGA, the accent is on positive thinking linked with the breathing exercises. In this Cosmic Breathing exercise, concentrate on inhaling positive qualities of love, peace and harmony, and exhaling negative thoughts of anger, envy, resentment and greed. Here are the directions:

1. Stand erect with legs together and arms held relaxed at sides. Inhale, and, at the same time, raise both arms straight out in front of you until they are parallel to the floor at shoulder height, elbows straight, fingers straight and together, palms pointing to the floor.

2. Exhale, bringing the arms sidewards at right angles to the body, still at shoulder level, palms down.

3. In one sharp motion, bend the hands at the wrists until fingers point toward the ceiling. The hands are now at right angles to the arms.

4. Inhale, slowly raise the eyes toward the ceiling and at the same time bring the hands upward in a semicircular motion until the middle fingers touch about 4 to 6 inches above the eyes, palms up.

5. Exhale, pushing the palms toward the ceiling. Make this an extreme stretching motion, stretching both the arms and the spine. The eyes are still focused on the backs of the hands at this point.

6. Inhale, slowly bringing the face back to original position and bringing the arms back to the same position they were in after completing Step 3. Arms are parallel to the floor, fingers pointing toward the ceiling.

7. In one sharp movement, bend the hands at the wrists until fingers are pointing toward the floor.

8. Exhale while bringing the straightened arms downward toward the floor.

9. When the extended fingers are about a foot apart, begin inhaling as the arms continue toward each other. Continue inhaling, and begin pointing fingers toward the ceiling so that you can place the hands together, back to back, fingers pointed to ceiling. Raise the hands together in this position until they are just under the chin.

10. Exhale as you reverse the hands so fingers point toward the floor and bring the hands down toward the floor still back to back. The hands will part naturally at a certain point, and the arms should be brought back to the sides of the body, hands bent at the wrists, palms facing the floor.

Repeat the entire exercise three times.

Craig Voelkert dances a part of Psalm 43..."Then shall I go to the altar of God,
to the God of my joy!"

Movement Prayers

After trying the CENTERING exercise you may wish to continue with some PRAYER GESTURES. Think of these as meditations or experiences rather than as exercises.

> In a sitting, kneeling or standing position,
> with eyes closed and body centered, extend
> your hands comfortably in front of you with
> palms facing up. Sense the life energy that
> you somehow hold in your hands. Let your
> prayer grow within you...not so much in words,
> as in the whole breathing, feeling, lifting of
> your body and thoughts.

> *"Give thanks to the Lord, for He is good,*
> *His love is everlasting!"*   Ps. 136:1

> *"In Him we live and move and have our being."*   Acts 17:28

How would you move-out the feeling of THANKFULNESS?

How would you move-out PRAISE or OFFERING? Try them in different ways.

The gesture for prayer that has become so common in the West is the tightly clasped hands. We have inherited this position from an old Germanic tradition. When a man entered the House of God, he withdrew his hand from his ever-ready sword. He clasped his sword hand and placed himself trustfully in God's care. The gesture has now come to mean piety, humbleness, contrition or a pulling together of our thoughts. It is an important gesture, but it is only one way to pray.

The early Christians prayed with arms extended in a cross. They faced the possibility of death for their following of Christ.

> Create a movement-statement with your hands for expressing the
> great affirmation of faith, AMEN. Take time to try it in
> several ways. Try it with eyes closed and then with eyes open.

> How would you move-out an ALLELUIA?
> Create a series of three ALLELUIA movements in joyous praise.
> How would you say and move ALLELUIA in a time of great sorrow?

The main point in these experiences is to understand that MOVEMENT-PRAYERS must come from within you. There is no right or wrong way. It must really be an expression that grows from your own searchings and sensings. The phrases should be short and should mean something to you personally. The Scripture quotations above are just suggestions to help you get started. The Psalms are rich in vivid imagery and beautiful prayer phrases of a timeless quality. Contemporary writing may be more appropriate for some. Others may have no need for words. Sometimes it is enough to simply offer your weakness, confusion, frustration or joy.

When Does Movement Become Dance?

Dance is the evolution of motion. All of life is in motion. We all begin in motion. The dancer is an embodiment of the cosmic motion that is around and within us.

Then, is all movement DANCE?

DANCE is movement set within a new time-space environment. "Measured, rhythmic motion" is one definition. The body seems to flow through the rhythmic patterns. Natural movement takes on the quality of pulsating energy. The instrument of the body is set apart from the ordinary, utilitarian actions. Dance movement is movement for its own sake. It is able to communicate feeling. This communication goes beyond the personal, yet it is rooted in the personal experience and creative inspiration of the dancer. The dancer is an artist of movement.

In tribal cultures everyone was able to enter into this realm of dance as expressive language. From childhood to old age, the evolution of dance was able to take place naturally as a whole-bodied, living art —a true celebration of being.

The situation today is quite different. Dancing is still an instinctive trait. The baby delights in moving. The small child dances with unselfconscious delight to rhythms and melodies. Singing games and dances are ways of relating to life and to other children. Circle dances and singing games have a socializing effect. If you want to learn something about the basic values of a society, watch the children play. Their songs and dances reflect the life goals of their parents in a singular way.

The stages of evolution of dance in contemporary Western society now become segmented. Dance for the older child and teenager is looked upon as social entertainment and a step to popularity. Some children receive dancing lessons. Dancing is limited to certain designated places and times. You go to a dance, when actually, you are the dance. It is much like the notion of "going to Church," when actually, you are the Church. Whenever something is removed from life, separated from the whole, it becomes external —something specialized, as opposed to something participated in. Too often, a DANCE becomes a means to something else. It is "used," with all that that word implies. When a dancer attempts to interpret life, pouring out an inner vision, it is difficult for people to get beyond the obstacles of their own preconceived ideas of dance. CREATIVE IMAGINATION is as necessary within the viewer as within the dancer for the DANCE to be fulfilled.

The DANCER, as communal spokesperson, has much to say to the world today, if it will but listen. The dancer gives outward form to that which is in each of us. The dancer can defy all that would pull us down. He or she is neither slave nor master, but simply one who gives abundantly. Like the musician, the dancer must of necessity give his art away. The more he gives it away, the more it is renewed. The more she loses her life, the more she finds it. SELF-centering becomes Centeredness for others.

The dancer is a witness to true freedom in life, the freedom which comes from within. The dancer shows us how to escape from the bondage of time. To dance is to live fully in the present moment with the freedom to act in new ways. This liberation is not just a freedom _from_ something, but a freedom _for_ something. Creativeness cannot be aimless or meaningless. Ecstasy is not gushing emotion or sentimentalism. The dancer recalls the emotion of the lived encounter, probes the deeper meanings and shapes it into understandable form. Ecstasy is an overwhelming spirit that empowers the dancer to go beyond acquired ability. He or she draws together the total experiences of a lifetime to dance the dance, rather than simply move out the steps.

A Dance Experience:

In the Spring of 1970 I was asked to present an Ecumenical Lenten Service in dance for churches in LaPorte, Indiana. The service was called "Beyond Words" and involved three dancers in addition to me.

One of the dancers had choreographed a strong protest dance in an afro-jazz style. The music used was a medley of Negro Spirituals by Morton Gould. A few intense slide projections built the context. In slave-march rhythm the dancer plodded up the center aisle of the church. The tempo began to pick up as she carried on the struggle into the chancel area. She became so much a physical and emotional part of that ache for freedom that her dance took on a power that had never before been realized. At one point she made an incredible leap from floor to top of altar steps. She danced "Beyond Words" and beyond herself. She _became_ the cry for justice.

The experience of that dance affected her so much that it resulted in her life commitment to dance. She majored in dance and theology in college and is continuing the work as a Danforth Scholar.

Not everyone in that conservative congregation "liked" the dance, but no one failed to get the meaning.

Dance perhaps cuts against some false values in contemporary society; not just by what it says, but also by what it is. The dancer gives fully in that one fleeting moment. The dance is not repeatable; it always has to be created anew. It is not a literal fact. It is not linear. It is not symmetrical. It is not any of the things that our technological world admires or rewards. Its very temporary, transient, lyrical quality has a preciousness about it that defies the values of our consumer culture.

The dancer moves freely, uncluttered by material possessions, while we cling to the weighty things of life. Creativeness is an ascent. The dancer moves...rising from earth to God, and in rising, tries to sweep the whole of creation with her. We, on the other hand, so often plod along on the middle ground.

The freedom of dance does not mean that dancers float in an ethereal, unreal world. Sometimes they must plunge into the anxieties, defeats and frustrations of life —feeling the suffering, as well as the joy, in every sinew and nerve.

The dancer suffers, fears and dies with humanity, but rises with a shout of "NEVERTHELESS!"

The DANCE is a gift to be shared.

FURTHER READING

Berdyaev, Nicolas, THE MEANING OF THE CREATIVE ACT, Collier Books, New York, 1962. *This is a significant work containing the forming and dominant ideas of the Russian religious philosopher, Berdyaev.*

Feldenkrais, Moshe, AWARENESS THROUGH MOVEMENT, Harper & Row, New York, 1973. *Dr. Feldenkrais writes of the importance of developing a good self-image through greater awareness. The book consists of practical health exercises for personal growth.*

Gunther, Bernard & Fusco, Paul, SENSE RELAXATION: BELOW YOUR MIND, Collier Books, New York, 1968. *A beautifully illustrated book offering simple sensory exercises for relaxing tension and toning the body.*

H'Doubler, Margaret H., DANCE: A CREATIVE ART EXPERIENCE, The University of Wisconsin Press, 1957. *A book dealing with the aesthetics of dance as related to the experience of teacher and student. She stresses the need for dance education in contemporary life.*

Mettler, Barbara, MATERIALS OF DANCE: AS A CREATIVE ART ACTIVITY, Mettler Studios, Tucson, Arizona, 1960. *A wealth of basic dance exercises and experiences that can be used with groups of any age. Each chapter covers a certain area of dance and contains enough material for any number of lessons. The purpose of the book is to make creative dance activity easy and enjoyable for anyone who wants it.*

Phenix, Philip H., EDUCATION AND THE WORSHIP OF GOD, The Westminster Press, Philadelphis, 1966. *His chapter on "Art as the Work of God" is especially important for developing a better understanding of the relationship of art and theology.*

Richards, M.C., CENTERING, in Pottery, Poetry and Person, Wesleyan University Press, Middletown, Connecticut, 1964. *While not dealing with dance specifically, CENTERING offers much stimulus for meditation. The ability to "center" oneself is very important for the creative dancer.*

Wigman, Mary, THE LANGUAGE OF DANCE, Translated from the German by Walter Sorell, Wesleyan University Press, Middletown, Connecticut, 1906 *This is the autobiography of a creative imagination rather than a life story. It gives a glimpse into the artistic process of creating dance and reveals the spiritual aspirations of a remarkable dancer and choreographer.*

Donna King and Debbie Kilhura, Anderson, Indiana Dance Workshop

Photograph by Michael A. Brown

chapter 3

DANCE
a journey into faith

Gayda Errett, Edmonton, Alberta.

Dance is more than a series of poses or gestures or steps. It is the
dynamic flow of human energies in time and space. It is fluid poetry
that cannot be contained. The camera can catch only that stop-action
glimpse, moment by moment. The dance is so much more than that.

To praise God in dance, is to offer Him the full measure of human
celebration.

What Is Religious Dance?

Everything that has been said about DANCE as an expressive art, applies without exception to the understanding of dance developed within a religious context. True dance grows from within. It may evolve gently. It may search and strain. It may burst with exuberance. But, whatever its character, it is always an energy, a tuning in on the motivating sources of life --not someone else's life --but your very own.

Dance communicates the human spirit. It breathes "soul" in every motion and emotion. When the dancer is filled with an urge to proclaim the action of God in his or her individual life, or in the life of the community --to offer and share God-given talents and enthusiasm in an extension of prayer, we have what can be rightly called RELIGIOUS DANCE. The term SACRED DANCE is used in reference to religious dance designed for use within a worship service. In some places, the name "Sacred Dance Choir" helped people to accept the idea of dance in the sanctuary. But the word, "sacred" has different meanings for different people.

One of the semantic difficulties that accompanies calling something "sacred" or "religious" is the fact that in our culture, these two words usually mean pious, reverent, untouchable, angelic, impersonal, stiff, formal, tedious, even difficult and painful. To combine the ideas of "sacred" and "dance" is almost too much for some people. We have been indoctrinated with this understanding of "religious" from Jansenism and Puritanism. "If it's fun, it must be a sin." It is all but impossible to fit the idea of "sacred dance" into this kind of religious mind-set. "Reverence" means whispering with bowed head and clasped hands.

Unfortunately, this mentality has led some dance leaders to make religious dance fit into the mold of "bowed head and clasped hands." It is really sad to see some of the examples of pious gesturing and posing given the name of Sacred Dance or Movement Choir. This is not to say that all Movement Choirs lack warmth and artistry. Some of them are very beautiful. But if the word "religious" is considered to be synonymous with "sanctimonious" and is expressed in cliché gestures, then dance becomes a travesty and only adds to the pathetic quality of some of our worship services. Equally sad is the type of religious dancing that is a pathetic gushing forth of subjective feelings before a captive audience. Neither of these two extremes touches upon the real meaning of religious dance.

Religious dance should be the very best that can be offered. It should not be attempted until it is carefully thought out and prepared. This means that the dancer or group of dancers is not only rehearsed well, but also knows the meaning and place the dance will have within the whole worship experience. The dance can then become authentic prayer in action.

It is not the music, or the form of the dance, or the subject matter, or the place in which the dance is performed, that makes it "religious." It is the whole motivation and intent of the action that makes it prayer, or offering, or praise. It is the personal commitment of the dancer to search out the meanings and conditions of existence, and through his or her particular talent, help us to see them in relation to God. You cannot dance a prayer or a conviction unless you truly affirm it with your entire being...unless you know who you are and what you believe in, or hope for, or love. An idea becomes immediate experience when it is given outward form in dance.

Contemporary Liturgical Dance, designed as part of a communal worship service or Mass, is a faith expression. It is not just a dance illustrating a hymn or poem, or a dramatization of a parable. It should expand the central idea and add a quality of living witness.

Liturgical Dance is very special. It should be used for those special times of celebration when it can touch the human spirit with its living gift. The congregation should be prepared to receive it as the special gift it is.

The following pages give us a glimpse into the heart of a dancer as she began to discover dance as a journey into faith. L'Ana Hyams Burton is a dancer, dance teacher and dance group leader for her church. She has written a paper entitled, "I Worship Through Dance." In it she recounts the experiences of her two years with dance at the United Church of Christ in Syosset, New York.

Thoughts of a Dancer   by L'Ana Hyams Burton

I began dancing as a very young child. When I was eighteen years old I knew that I would always dance. I know that at this point my dance training really began.

I had started going to Sunday school as a very young child and eventually I was baptized, confirmed and received as a full member of the church. I could then finally choose not to return. It was not until approximately eight years later, through teaching dance at the church, oddly enough, that I realized I did not know God. I realized that I had completely turned my back on any religious thoughts. Not only that, which in itself was hard enough to deal with, but I also found myself feeling indifferent as to whether or not God even existed.

I was fortunate to be around people who were warm and who welcomed my questions. Their guidance helped me to begin a long struggle to find out what I did believe. I have now come to see this struggle as a lifelong venture. Truthfully, at that time, the Bible, the church services, my readings, and my prayers, did not give me much help. I did feel one thing, which was unexplainable, yet which gave me assurance that there is a God. That one thing came straight from those people. They all had a special quality and a special love which I felt in their presence. It is the kind of quality which makes you feel lucky to know them and have them as friends. It seemed to me that right before me was living proof of God's existence. I saw a glow around those people which was as clear and certain to me as if God Himself were standing there before me. Somehow, it was not too important that I did not feel anything yet. Those people showed me something that I knew I had to find. There were times when everything else made me want to discontinue learning about Christianity. During such discouraging moments, one of those people would be nearby and, somehow, through the simplest of conversations, I could feel that special glow.

Six months later, my dancing and my religious struggle met one another. I found myself dancing my confusions and frustrations to God. It was a great release. No longer was it so emotionally frustrating, because I had found a way to communicate with God. I had heard something about sacred dance and had gone to see a sacred dance group perform, but I did not realize that what I was doing was sacred dance.

By chance, I was asked if I would like to perform the dance I had been working on, for a concert which my dance school was presenting. I did not think of this dance as a composition to be performed anymore than I thought I was doing "sacred dance." But, I became excited at the opportunity.

Several months later, we repeated the concert. This time the ministers from my church attended the performance. Later, after we discussed the idea of sacred dance many times, a date was set for my dance to become a part of a Sunday morning service. I spent as much time as possible working on the dance in the sanctuary, fitting it into a new and strange space. It was at that time that I wrote up the following notes to help clarify in my own mind what this dance meant. When it was ready to be viewed by the ministers, I brought them the notes. I thought that the notes would help them get a deeper insight into the dance. Under their suggestion, these notes became a part of the morning bulletin to be shared with the congregation:

Thoughts on "The Spiritual Moment"

"This dance is unique in that it is part of an actual religious experience, rather than only an interpretation of an experience. The creation of the dance itself and the religious experience cannot be separated. All future attempts I may make at expressing religion through dance will probably be choreographed from the perspective of a dancer. But this was not. I danced this one day almost spontaneously, as more of a contemplation--a conversation with God; not as a dance composed of steps set to music.

It was a discovery of a new and much clearer way for me to relate to God. Doing the dance left me with a feeling that something made sense. A feeling I hadn't felt at all during the seven months before, when I first had begun to think seriously about my feelings toward God. I was able to channel seven months of emotional feelings into something that I could relate to. I found that dance is a medium in which I can express feelings, doubts, faith, beliefs, anxiety...a direction for me to travel in.

The very first movements of the dance, although only lasting a few seconds, summarize what went on for seven months earlier. I did not know how I felt about God. I felt alone-frustrated-confused-doubtful. But then I ...

feel something: a breath from God/ I feel God's presence/ my hand/ God's touch is upon it.

From then on, the dance explores His presence, trying to see, learn and understand more. The dance ends at the beginning. There is a commitment to follow God. There is the statement:

Here I am. And I know you are here.

I have thought a great deal about those persons for whom dance is an unfamiliar or uncomfortable experience and how to make my message clearer or maybe more literal for them. But while working on a few verbal statements to be included with the dance, I found that I did not want to put that kind of clear-cut limitation on the interpretation. One of the miracles of the dance is that it has the power to express deep feelings which cannot be verbalized. I know that all of the verbal statements above have only been formulated because of the dance. I couldn't have written any of this without it. For me, as dancer, attaching words destroys the freedom of movement. I am so lucky to have this opportunity. I feel so thankful for the chance to share this in part of the worship service...FOR ME, and for many others."

The Ministry of Dance

Through this worship experience, I learned that this was where I wanted to dance. At that point, dance became a larger part of my life. I had significantly greater incentive to study because I knew that the more technique I could master, the larger my movement vocabulary would be. Most importantly, I knew that I wanted to dance in the church again.

I needed to do an enormous amount of preparing before I would feel ready to dance in church. I had only danced this composition on a bare stage with lighting, then transferred it to the sanctuary. I slowly became aware of the distinct differences there are between the two. I felt that space is an important area of concern that needs to be considered in sacred dance, and often is not. The techniques of the performer are in one way a great asset whether performing for an audience or communicating to a congregation.

The Dance Artist

An artist of the dance has a unique background to bring to sacred dance. Often what the dancer is trying to project is just not there, because the craft is not. When one performs on the stage there is an atmosphere created in which the dancer is free to become something he is not. Bright lights, costumes, make-up and a darkened audience are all aids for the dancer. The aura of the stage has a special, magical excitement about it. I can best describe the experience as feeling a warm glow projected onto your body from the lighting, a vibrant characterization from the make-up, and an intense feeling of power from the darkness of a hushed audience. Knowing of these experiences, I think every performer is overwhelmed by stage fright immediately before stepping out onto the stage. Much of the fear comes from the stark realization that at that moment you are alone. Once you step out on the stage it is up to no one but yourself. The experienced performer will become that character he is to portray. Therefore, the fear disappears. The atmosphere which becomes the professional dancer's entire life is an unreal, magical, mysterious and make-believe existence, in this sense.

It is so different when you are dancing in the sanctuary. At a worship service the entire atmosphere is not theatrical. I was worried about that because I felt that the lack of familiar surroundings would inhibit me. On the contrary, I felt completely relaxed without the unrealness of make-up, applause, and the airy attitude of the artist. I have never felt dance become so real with life. I sat with the congregation, and after dancing, sat down again, as a part of the congregation. The performance atmosphere was broken. I felt naturally a part of the service. I understood the progression of the service, so that by the time I rose to dance, I was very inspired, full of joy, and very much aware of God. For the first time, I knew that I understood something about worship. I was truly worshipping God. The emotion I experienced at that moment was a combination of love, awe and joy.

I felt a nervous and excited joy, yet, my nervousness was of a different nature than stage fright. I did not feel alone at all. I had the sensation of not being alone while I danced. God's presence filled the entire church. I felt a strong support which gave me strength and warmth. Instead of a staged transformation into an unreal character, I was simply myself. The thoughts I projected were from within me. The majority of themes a performer tries to express come from sources other than from within oneself. I doubt if there is anything more rewarding for the artist than to be dancing out something from within his or her very soul.

What I have learned about dance as a performer, regardless of the vast differences between performance on a stage and dance in worship, has been vital in my ability to understand the artistry of communication and projection.

Movement Communication

All people involved in movement communication (and I would add especially those who are dancing for a congregation,) need to learn about communication through projection. Although it must come from deep within, the way you move, how you appear, and how you use your facial expression, are qualities which, nevertheless, need to be studied. They are minute, intricate techniques which are essential for projection. There must be more than a desire to dance in worship. The artist takes this for granted, while others need to be shown how important training is. No one would ever think of volunteering to play the organ on Sunday for the service unless he was trained with some knowledge of the instrument. Why should a person who has no dance training expect to be able to communicate to a congregation through dance? Unfortunately, through no fault of their own, it seems that this is an art where people are led to believe they can simply form a dance group and dance in their church.

I do not completely disagree with sacred dance which involves persons who are not trained dancers. I am simply trying to stress the importance of technique. There is so much emphasis placed on forming ideas, finding attractive costumes, and using appropriate music. If there were more emphasis placed on how to get our bodies better prepared, these other problems would fall into place. Unless there is a shift in emphasis, many people will continue to view sacred dance as an embarrassing and indecent faltering of barefoot dancers.

During a week-long Celebration Seminar at a retreat house in Edmonton, Alberta, ministers, religious educators, musicians, dancers and media people came together to learn and create in one another's art. The intensive inter-mix enabled dancers to create music, media people to dance, ministers to use media, and educators to teach through banners, song and dance. It is this kind of sensitivity to the work and struggle of the creative process that unites people in a Spirited enterprise and deepening faith. Giving bodily form to one's belief, accompanied by original music, was a thrilling experience for this group.

Gayda Errett introduced dance, as religious expression, into her church a few years ago. Since then, she has organized a Liturgical Dance Group which is often asked to perform in other churches in the province of Alberta.

Gayda has found dance to be a most fluent language for expressing her love for God and her joy in living. In her own words:

> "I believe God has revealed to me at various turning points in my life that His Glory is Here and Now and is manifested when I live my life to proclaim His Spirit in me (despite my human frailties).

> "I believe that to proclaim God's Spirit dwelling in all of us is to live in accord with His Divine Intentions: 'to be in Harmony with God - with myself - with others and with the earth'.   (Quote from Bethel Bible Series)

> "I believe the Glory of God - like the Kingdom of Heaven, is at hand and becomes so, when I 'Live' out in fullness a 'God-filled' life. I believe I become more 'fully alive'!

> "My 'aliveness' is my statement of faith and I try to 'celebrate' this wherever I go."

From Darkness to Light

For a Holy Saturday Vigil Service, a liturgical dance group combined with the choir and instrumentalists to perform the "Missa Samba" by Alexander Peloquin. The "Gloria" and the "Sanctus" were jubilantly danced to the rhythms of bells and drums. This was a midnight service. At the time of the "Gloria" special lights gradually flooded the sanctuary, filling it with glory in sound, color and movement.

A Mass at St. Thomas the Apostle Catholic Church in Chicago, Illinois.

FURTHER READING

Bruce, V.R. & Tooke, J.D. Lord of the Dance: An Approach to Religious Education. Pergamon Press, New York, 1966.

Eliade, Mircea. The Sacred and the Profane. Harper Torchbooks. Harper & Row, New York, 1961. (paperback)

Oesterly, W.O.E. The Sacred Dance: A Study in Comparative Folklore. Macmillan, New York, 1923.

Taylor, Margaret (Chaney). A Time to Dance, Symbolic Movement in Worship. Originally published by United Church Press, Boston in 1967. Revised and reprinted in 1976 by The Sharing Company, P.O. Box 190, North Aurora, IL 60542.

This book gives a fine historical background of the development of dance and movement choirs in liturgy.

Wosien, Maria-Gabriele. Sacred Dance - Encounter with the Gods. Avon Books, London, England, 1974.

A beautifully illustrated history of sacred dance as it relates to the religions of the world. It charts mankind's spiritual journey.

Kathy Iverson-Beckman and Rebecca Thompson, Pacific Lutheran University
Liturgical Dance Ensemble.

chapter 4

designing dance for

...LITURGY

by KATHY IVERSON-BECKMAN

Without ecstasy there is no dance.

Without form there is no dance.

Dance gives form to ecstasy.

Kathy Iverson-Beckman

Kathryn Iverson-Beckman is a graduate of Stanford University, with a major in English, and extra-curricular involvements in Orchesis, a Stanford dance ensemble, and the Lutheran Student Association. She received her Masters degree in dance from the University of Southern California. She has taught at the University of Redlands, California; at the State University of New York-Stony Brook, and at the Pacific Lutheran University, Washington. Her dance workshops have been presented in Washington, Oregon, Minnesota, Illinois, California and Canada. Together with five members of the Pacific Lutheran University Liturgical Ensemble, she presented a workshop in Liturgical Dance for the 1973 Conference of Worship and the Arts, in Minnesota. Kathy continues to create in dance at Pacific Lutheran University. She is not only a vivacious and gifted dancer, she is a delightful person who can share her enthusiasm joyously with others.

What Is There to CELEBRATE?

... And How Do We Do It?

by Kathy Iverson-Beckman

When we decide to choreograph a dance for the worship service, we hope that it will bring a special dimension to the service and we want that dimension to "work" for the congregation. We want it to be the most beautiful and moving experience we can offer. We want it to touch the people deeply, to reach out and to bring them into the dance experience, figuratively, and sometimes, even literally. We become the planners of celebration —— the careful designers of an experience that we hope will have vitality of a spontaneous experience. Yet, all planners know, or soon discover, that "spontaneity" needs help in most situations. If we do well in our preparations, perhaps we can enable a celebration to happen. Between the first insight which starts the planners planning and the final event lie many hours of preparation.

One of the first things we face is the whole concept of celebration:
What causes us to celebrate? How can we turn to celebration with the
horrendous threats and events of our time? How can we spend our energies on seemingly extracurricular activities like Dance when the
very core of our lives seems to be in such upheaval?

At the heart of the Faith is Praise. If we can keep it central in our
lives, we are not overcome by the pressures and the fears. We cannot
ignore the pain and the ugliness. We see the sorrow, but we can also
see the beauty, and we must make space in our lives for the beauty, or
we will become blind to it. Celebration and praise come out of our
lives, in the full face of everything that is horrible and everything
that is beautiful. We start here, where we, the particular planners,
dancers, choreographers, are when we begin our creative endeavors.

Before you are a dancer, or a poet, or a musician, you are a person.
Bring to your art the richness of your own experience. Dance about
those things that are important to you. It is difficult to choreograph on a theme that is too general or abstract. The work becomes
meaningful to you, and to those who dance in it or watch it, as you
give it particular meaning.

Celebration is not necessarily equated with exuberance. Our faith
recognizes the struggles, hurts, sorrows of God's people as well as
the joys and blessings. There is a peace that has to do with a con-
frontation with the truth, and a joy that does not laugh. We look
into our own lives and begin the choreography as our own offering,
designing not necessarily happy dances, yet not necessarily sad ones
either. We give form to what we value expressing from the heights
or the depths of our experience.

The most important thing about our work is the attitude we bring to
it. When we dance in a worship service, we are performing in the
sense of personally giving form to an idea (a literal or non-literal
idea). It is not a time to dazzle a congregation with our technique,
but it is a time to embody our insights for the enrichment of the congregation and to the glory of God.

That point became very clear to me some years ago as I was walking
with a fellow teacher at the University of Redlands. My dance group
had just been a part of a chapel service, and my friend commented that
she had greatly enjoyed watching the dancers. Then she said this surprising thing. She said that although she loved dancing, she, of
course, couldn't dance herself because one of her arms was withered.
It rocked me back on my heels. Here was a lady whose entire personality "danced," and yet, in a very particular way, our dancing gave her
a chance to move vicariously and kinesthetically through us. We were,

in a very real sense, dancing in her place. A humbling and wonderful
thought stripped us of all arrogance! If our talent is dancing, then
let us rejoice in the power of dancing. There are so many who cannot
dance. We who can, may dance for them.

When we decide to bring a dance into the liturgy we are saying something
about our understanding of dance and our understanding of worship. Dance
and worship are loaded words that can evoke strong reactions from people.
Both can be profound experiences or trivial ones. I have seen people
throw together "a little something" for a worship service, and I have
seen people throw together "a little something" to serve as worship.
If we regard dance as a trivial activity, "a little something" for a
special service next week because dance is currently "in", then all we
will get will be "a little something" which the congregation will more
or less endure.

Ah, but there is so much more! As a teacher once said to me: "to dance
is to sing the highest kind of melody ——a silent melody sung by the inner voice within the soul of man." The creative process happens at our
core, not on the periphery. It is not an easy process, as any composer
of music or writer of sermons knows. If you let the creative process have
full reign, it will result in a product of beauty and significance. The
arts can increase our abilities to see and hear and feel and, consequently, to understand and appreciate more in our world. They involve
us in an enormous and constant encounter with life, and help us to find
new ways of seeing. The arts can work hand in hand with the worship to
help us get beyond ourselves and our self-indulgences and self-insistings.
In the creative process we are probing our own resources and trying to
be alive to the concreteness of the moment. Such a process provides so
many insights into our lives!

The goal of Dance in worship is to bring a religious dimension to both
the dancing and the liturgy. Both Dance and Worship are sometimes brush-
ed off as frivolous, extra activities and yet to us, who value both, they
are at the center of our concerns. We are really dancing when we commit
our concentration, joy and zest to the dance. It would be wonderful to
incorporate movement into worship so that it is not just a current curi-
osity, but so that it makes us a more dancing people. We long for a
fusion of our minds and bodies and emotions and perceptions to give the
process of our living a religious dimension.

Pacific Lutheran Dance Ensemble at the closing Celebration, Minneapolis
Conference on Worship and the Arts, 1973.

Designing Dance for Liturgy

<u>The Particulars of the Process</u>

Dance can add a powerful visual dimension to religious expression. That
visual dimension becomes a spiritual one as well when the dance really
works. The vital energy of the body, used to give form to an idea, is a
gift —an offering of the spirit. You cannot dance out that which you do
not believe.

Dance is a visual expression. It appeals to the sense of sight, and the
sense of sight is a very strong sense. We retain longer what we see than
what we hear. Consequently, what you do in your dance is going to make
an impression. We can be very self-conscious about people dancing. It
is important that what is done, be done well. If not, the congregation
will fail to see your message, and will instead be embarrassed for you.
They may not have seen any other dance in a service, and may reject it as
a viable form of religious expression if it is not well done.

It takes time to make the dance exciting to watch. It also takes some insight into the process of putting dances together. There are many superb books on the choreographic process, and increasingly, schools offer courses in dance technique and choreography. This chapter will serve as a springboard with the hope that it will spark your interest to explore other sources.

You should allow time for the choreographic process, especially if you are just beginning. A four or five minute dance should probably take you about twenty-five hours to choreograph and rehearse. It is wise to begin with a small number of dancers, and the movement should be fairly simple so that everyone will know the movements well and be able to move as an ensemble. A well-rehearsed piece will give your dancers confidence. With confidence they can get past their self-consciousness and get into the dance. Giving your dancers enough time in rehearsal is the biggest favor you can do for them and the dance.

Each person, dancer or non-dancer, will come with his own idea of what "dance" is. You, as director, will have to help your people develop the movement resources they already have, as well as to expand their movement vocabulary. Movement comes from the inside out. When people first begin dancing they usually try to look like dancers, and are too concerned with the external line and pose. You should help them feel like dancers. Get them moving. The motivation for a movement is at the center of the dancer's body, even when just the arms are moving. What is made physical and visible comes from the non-physical and invisible.

It is very difficult to evaluate a person's grasp of movement and dance until you see that person move. It is not always an advantage to have years of training if that training has trapped you in the technique and not expanded your own creative abilities. Nearly every time a student comes in with excellent-sounding credentials, I am reminded that years of training do not necessarily give the ability to know what makes movement interesting to watch. When you begin a group, you also begin a kind of movement training. Try to develop some common insights into the use of dance. Work to develop an ensemble: people who can move well together and who know what movement can mean. Your task is to put life into movement and eliminate affectations. It may take longer with people who are new to dance, but if they are motivated and persevere, the results can be exciting!

In planning the rehearsal session, include warm-up activities and work on some particular movement techniques before you begin on the rehearsal of the particular piece. Consider the warm-up activities as performance exercises. As you do pliés and brushes and swongs, do them with an awareness of the space all around you —not only the space in front, but over your head, on your neck, behind your shoulders. Work for a sense of total movement, even when the movement seems to be just an exercise. You make it into more than calisthenics by the level of concentration and fullness you bring to it.

Be "dancing" even in the small moments of the beginning of your sessions, for it is here that you set the tone for your work. You can still make your efforts fun while you work hard. Your sessions are not only to rehearse the piece, but to compose it and to prepare the body that will dance it.

There are several things you can do to develop your basic idea and draw out of your dancers more articulate and refined movement. By focusing on the three elements of movement: the spatial design, use of time, and the use of energy, you can provide an enormous amount of material for all levels of dancers.

Spatial design can be thought of in terms of the size of the movement (small, medium and large), the level (low, middle, high), the direction (forward, backward, diagonal, sideways, turning) in relation to the dancer's body and in relation to the front, side and diagonal directions of the room.

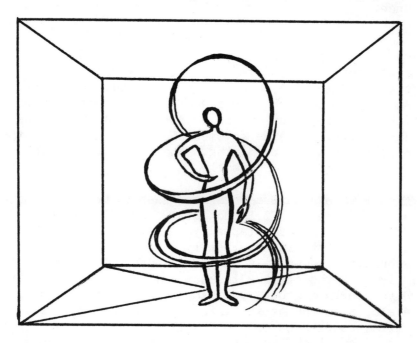

A simple movement phrase could be varied in terms of size, the direction you are facing, where you are located in space. Each of these elements affects not only your dancing, but how the movement sequence is perceived by the congregation.

PRACTICE using SPACE:

Design a simple movement phrase; define the spatial elements you are using. Where does it move in space? Is the design symmetric or asymmetric? Try doing the sequence on a different level. Make the movements smaller. Include a contrast in the direction, space design, or level, and see how that alters your phrase. Develop five or six such variations on your original theme.

Time, like space, is something to be worked with. Sub-categories of Time include duration (the length of your dance, or of phrases within the dance), the rate of speed (fast or slow), and the use of rhythm (the underlying beat and the rhythmic groupings around the beat).

PRACTICE with TIME:

>Try your sequence twice as fast as originally
>designed. Try it twice as slow. What is the
>important part of the study? Phrase the piece
>to emphasize the important ideas and movements.
>Move simultaneously, the whole body performing
>the movements. Then sequentially, one hand,
>then a shoulder, your upper back, a heel, an
>ear lobe...one body part at a time. Become
>aware of time as an element of movement. Be-
>come aware of part of your body you don't nor-
>mally notice.

When discussing the third element of movement, Energy, we refer to the quality or dynamic of the movement. Use of energy involves the whole body. While your arm is moving, your spine is alert, your heel attentive. Exert the force with strength or lightness, and at the same time, try to eliminate unnecessary tension.

PRACTICE in the use of ENERGY:

>Explore the different uses of energy: a sustained
>flowing movement; a percussive, sharp movement;
>movement that is swinging or that is vibratory;
>forceful and slow; forceful and fast; light and
>slow; light and fast.

There are many choices. What finally appears in your dance should happen because you have chosen it to happen, not because you weren't aware of alternatives.

As yet, we have not talked about "meaning." You will find that movement is full of connotations. Once you have the tools of your craft, you can work for the subtleties of meaning. Minor changes in the way a movement is done enormously change the meaning of a movement as it is perceived by a congregation.

An understanding of the elements of movement extends your resources. It helps you to use movement more consciously. If there is no variation in these, the piece will be dull, somewhat like a bland meal with food that is all the same color and texture and temperature. These elements of Space, Time and Energy all come to life with proper motivation. Where does this motivation come from? It can come out of the movement itself or out of your attitude toward the movement.

In the final analysis, if you have a good sense of the phrasing in your movement, and if you do it so that it projects out to the congregation, you will have something meaningful. Your particular message will come across clearly. A good phrase is usually as long as a breath of air in a speaking phrase, and a dance consists of many phrases. Each phrase should have organic unity and should be important to the whole statement of the dance.

The love of the dance is finally manifest in the dancing —the kinesthetic phrases and the projection that sends them out to those watching. Do you "project" your movement, not only to the back of the church, but clear past the wall into the parking lot? Or does it look as though there were a glass barrier between you and the congregation, and you are oblivious that anyone is watching? The pastor projects his voice, and so includes us in his ideas. The same way, we project our movement so that it will be clear to the congregation and include the congregation in the Dance.

Beginning efforts tend to be very static, often because the dancers are moving from pose to pose, instead of in phrases of dynamic movement. Beginners also tend to have an inward focus that pushes away the congregation instead of a projection that includes the congregation. Projection is psychic as well as physical. A dancer with projection can make standing still exciting.

The creative process will make many demands on you. It will make you consciously use the craft of choreography to develop a lovely artistic moment. Part of the process is conscious work. At the same time, there is also the need to be alive to the dynamic relationships that may happen accidently in rehearsal —an instant of lucky improvisation or a lucky "mistake" that captures the spark you might otherwise work hours to develop. Take care in the rehearsal. Many dances have been beaten into monotony by wrenching beautiful movements into a countable sequence for the sake of teaching it. When you analyze and break down the movement for teaching, be careful not to control the life out of it. The life exists between and through the counts —the wonderful connecting energy that makes 1...2...3...4...vital, instead of static.

In a few words, some advice, then:

Begin simply, with enough contrast in the rhythm, spatial design and use of energy to give it life. Work on details, the focusing of the eyes, the position of the hands, the precision in the timing. Work on entrances and exits. Pay attention to how you get up and down, because as soon as you are visible, you have begun the dance. From that point, there should be no "private moments" of brushing wisps of hair from the face or tugging on costumes. Surround the dance with a frame of concentrated silence.

· simplicity
· careful attention to detail
· confident entrances and exits
· a framework of silence

Furthermore: Begin with unison dances.
              Add variation in timing (in a round or canon)
              Add variation in spatial design (use of level and
                            changes of direction)

              Later, as you gain choreographic skill and insight,
                   you can do dances choreographed with several
                   different parts.
              Simplicity is the key, for the sake of those who
                   dance and for the sake of those who watch.

                   And, SIMPLICITY isn't simple to achieve.

Finally, remember that you are dancing on behalf of the congregation.
You are moving for them, in the sense of "in their place," just as the
minister is often moving on behalf of the congregation. Therefore, dance
with a fullness that comes from enough rehearsal, an awareness of the elements of movement, dynamic phrasing and projection. Love it enough so
that you can dance the Dance.

Kathy Iverson-Beckman and the Liturgical Dance Ensemble combine
with liturgist and choirs for the Invocation at the President's
Council for Physical Fitness Clinic, Pacific Lutheran University,
1973.

Post Script:

Liturgy means "the work of the people." In order for the "people" to be open to anything new in a service, they need to be prepared. There was a time when significance was equated with how much people could get involved in something. If the congregation could be up and moving, the thinking went, the event would be more significant for them, than if they just sat and watched. Physical involvement does not necessarily give the activity significance. As a society, we are not a dancing people, alas. If the congregation is to, in fact, do the movements, you must carefully prepare them and give them some options. Otherwise, they are apt to feel threatened and manipulated. If they are to watch, assure them of the spirit of your presentation and validate the importance of their watching attitude.

A few words before the service begins can do a great deal to help the congregation participate in the Dance. I try to include the following remarks when speaking to a congregation that has not had dance in the service before:

> Movement is already a significant part of the service. The minister moves symbolically on our behalf. We participate by actively watching. The choir presents music on our behalf. We may not actually be singing, but through their voices, we are also raised in song. In dance, too, we perform in the sense of "personally giving form" to our ideas, and we do it on the behalf of all gathered here. Through the dancers, the congregation may also join in the dance.

> Dance is one of the "liberating arts" —long recognized as one of man's first art forms. In our culture, we have become dis-integrated. We have become verbally oriented at the expense of the many non-verbal ways of receiving knowledge. Dance, along with the other arts such as music, sculpture, painting, extends our non-verbal dimensions and integrates our physical abilities with our intellectual and aesthetic ones. A renewed interest in Dance across the country illustrates the effort to integrate our lives again, to fuse our abilities to move and think and feel into a powerful and rich creative expression.

FURTHER READING

Cheney, Gay and Strader, Janet, The Modern Dance. Allyn and Bacon, Inc.,
    Boston. 85 pages. (paperback)

A beautifully written paperback that gives an excellent philosophical
as well as practical approach to choreography and technique. The
"Learning Experiences" included in the chapters are especially helpful.

Humphrey, Doris, The Art of Making Dances. Grove Press, Inc., New York.
    189 pages. (paperback)

The first book to give guidelines for choreography —an important
and extremely helpful book.

Ellfeldt, Lois, A Primer for Choreographers. National Press Books, Palo
    Alto, California. (paperback)

A Primer, in fact. Many of my students like the specific suggestions
and insights into the process of choreography.

Turner, Margery J., The New Dance. University of Pittsburgh Press,
    Pittsburgh, PA. 128 pages. (hardbound)

An excellent approach to non-literal dance, with specific assignments
to sharpen the skills of all choreographers. It includes chapters on
Music and Dance, and Lighting for Dance.

Ellfeldt, Lois, and Carnes, Edwin, Dance Production Handbook Or Later Is
    Too Late. National Press Books, Palo Alto, California. 220 pages.

This paperback is geared to dance concerts, but can be helpful to
liturgical dance desiring special lighting, costumes and staging, or
for setting up special church pageants.

Sherbon, Elizabeth, On the Count of One: A Guide to Movement and Progression
    in Dance. National Press Books, Palo Alto, California. (paperback)

A creative approach to technique and composition.

The books listed above are in order of recommendation and probable value.

chapter 5

MIME

a language of the heart

The Art of MIME

Mime is an art expression that lies between dance and drama. It is
a symbolic language akin to the gestures used in far-eastern dancing.
It is an art that creates illusions of gravity, space, fluidity, push
and pull, not just for the sake of technique, but to draw us into the
imaginative style of the artist and thereby into our own imaginations.
Communication within silence is the world of mime.

Mime can capsulize time or stretch it out endlessly. It can touch
birth, maturity and death with a few gestures of the body. With humor
and reverence, it can approach the mystery of life itself.

When I first began to gather the ideas for this book, I thought of the
memorable examples of dance and movement that I had experienced. The
mimes of Marcel Marceau were among the images that appeared immediately.
He is, without doubt, the best known and the greatest of mimes in the
world today. Each performance reaches a peak of artistry and total
personal investment. In his concert program book, Marcel speaks of
his great love for mime from childhood on. As a boy, he was enchanted
by the antics of Charlie Chaplin who could make people laugh one minute
and cry the next. No matter what misfortune might knock him down, he
would rise triumphant in the end, to travel on in his own jaunty way
down the road of life.

Marcel has dedicated his life to the art of mime ——"truly a language
of the heart" as he calls it. "Everything can be expressed through the
art of mime," he says. Where words can be deceitful and set up barriers
of misunderstanding, mime, in order to be understood, must be clear and
simple. It speaks to all. It is a universal art, a means of communication between all people who seek love and beauty.

Within the space of silence, Marcel portrays the human being in his most
secret yearnings. Sometimes he is the beloved Bip, wearing his striped
pull-over and his battered stovepipe hat with the trembling flower perched
on top. Bip, as the silent observer of our lives and loves, our joys and
sorrows, is ever-pursuing his dreams, though never missing a butterfly
on the way.

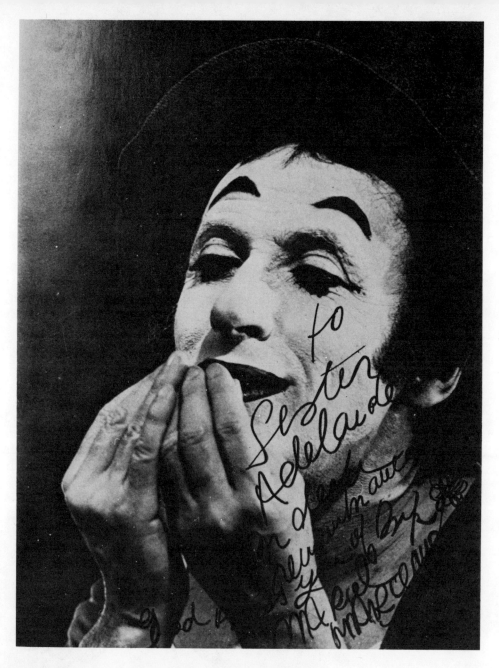

An Interview with MARCEL MARCEAU

In February of 1975, I had the privilege of interviewing Marcel Marceau.
He was on the campus of Purdue University for an evening performance and
had just received a standing ovation from 6,000 people in the Hall of
Music. When I introduced myself to him and explained the work of The Center For Contemporary Celebration and my own personal work in designing
dance and mime for the liturgy, Marcel's face lit up and he began to talk
with growing enthusiasm. I asked him if he would speak about his art and
the sources of his inspiration for the mimes. The religious dimension of
mime seemed to be a subject that delighted him. The feeling of "interview"
vanished as he spoke from his heart. Marcel, the world renowned artist,
was Marcel, the warmly human, fellow traveler. Much of his thought was
conveyed by facial expressions and gestures. He spoke in French, at times,
but most of the conversation was in English.

As a jumping off point, I mentioned that three of his mimes particularly
impressed me as powerful statements of man's religious experience. I have
included a brief sketch of each of these.

The Creation of the World

An expression of the Genesis account of the creation of the world, from the beginning, through the experience of Adam and Eve in the garden to their expulsion and their taking on the burdens and the nobility of work. Marcel seems to become, totally, the spiritual energy of creation.

Bip in the Modern and Future Life

Bip, the clown, the dreamer awake, finds himself going through the stages of the evolution of the human mind. He tries to cope with technology. With the vision of a Teilhard de Chardin, he enters inter-planetary space and walks off into the future reaches of the universe to touch eternity.

The Hands

In this mime, the two hands become the two polarities or tensions within each individual person ——the capacity for good or evil, reason or passion. The struggle between the two is first defined, then there is intense conflict. Powerful facial expressions, alternating from one to the other of the opposing forces, contributes to the drama otherwise created by the hands alone. In the end, the battle is resolved and balance gains control.

He first spoke of the mime "The Creation of the World":

Marcel: "When you play the lonely performer, you reach for symbolism.
The Creation of the world is easy to understand, for everybody
who has a background in catechism, will have heard the story.
Every child, even if he is not religious later, learns the
Bible stories. I took the symbols, there, you know, the hands
creating....the elements of creation....the snake....the apple
(Marcel's hands sculptured all these symbols so visibly in the
air, as he spoke, that I felt as if he were a magician actually
producing them out of thin air). It is very important to rely
upon symbols with which the public can identify upon the recollection of Genesis.

"I found out something that is very moving: the 'Creation of
the World' has been shown on French television, and it was
beautifully done, with close-ups and so forth. It had such
an impact on peasants of France, especially those people who
are close to the earth, that they were absolutely smashed
(astonished) by it. In a sense, it did me much good, because
suddenly it brought consciousness to people about an awareness
of the creation of man.

"I think the most important thing is 'what is religion?' After all,
it is for me to believe in man...in certain principles which are
moral...of behavior of man in search for his identity...in search
of love...in search of knowledge of himself and his earth. Have
you read Teilhard de Chardin? You see, I agree very much with
him in many things he says...the example that the supernatural,
that God is in us and makes...a super-sensitivity...that is
what makes us create...you see. And I think that I did the
"Creation of the World" not only from the cosmology and from the
Bible, but I was inspired by a force which came to me and I cannot explain how it came. This is a great example of how inspiration is a secret force...which is knowing grace, knowing God...
naming God, naming spiritual forces. The poetry was combined
with music. I chose, of course, Mozart...because it was a beautiful combination...flow of movement, music and signs.

"Cain and Abel is another Bible mime which I once did, but Cain
and Abel is very difficult, you see. With a group it would be
easier. It is very difficult to show Abel giving a sheep to
God. The public would laugh, you see (in gesture, he petted
the wooly lamb and then raised it in offering). You see, as
beautiful as it is with words, I changed the interpretation of
the Bible, because if I use the Bible story as written, Cain does
not come through. I do not do this mime anymore. You have to
explain so much.

"The one pantomime which would be fantastic to do is the Crucifixion.
This would be very interesting to do. I must tell you something
frankly, I thought for years and years to play the Passion. I
would call it, 'Passion... la Inquisition...le Descent de Tombeau...

la Resurrection.' This could be very strong.

"You know, I think I have had an influence on the young people. In Godspell, for instance, the gesture (he spread his arms in the form of a cross, the movements he had used at the end of 'Creation of the World'), I'm sure that Bip the clown had an influence on Godspell, even though they don't recognize it. Even Jesus Christ Superstar was probably inspired from the Passion Plays of the Middle Ages that inspired me.

"But to make a white face out of Christ...which is not disturbing at all, because we are 'the fool of God', 'fou de Dieux', this makes him universal. The clown is man with all the absurdities, the beauty, the comedy, the tragedy and all the foolishness of humanity. Passion Plays have been played for centuries and centuries. I have invented nothing.

"I think that the whole ceremony of liturgy is a pantomime, because the signs of language...to bless...to give (he made the gesture used at Mass), the whole ritual is pantomime and a beautiful way of education.

"Of course you know, and don't forget it, that the great art of the Bible is literature...the writing...it is the way it is written. It is really the holy writing...but the gesture is very important also...because each word is a key, and every gesture has a symbol. You have it in the Agnus Dei (Lamb of God)...the lift up your hearts. You have it in the Orthodox religion with all the bows and blessings.

"In 'The Hands', you remember. I chose Russian liturgical music. One day a woman came to see me. She was Orthodox Russian and she was offended. She said, 'How can you do this? How can you take the Russian Church music? It belongs to us.' I said, 'No, God doesn't belong to you. Your religion belongs to you, as a believer. If I want to choose your songs because they touched my heart, God will understand what I do. You have no right to tell me what I can do or not do. I do it because I feel inspired and I love to do it.' She couldn't say anything. She was absolutely rigid. She was an orthodox woman who was shocked that I would play her religious music on the stage. She thought it should only be for the church.

"What is church? It is a show. It is a celebration. It is like theatre. It does not reject the thought of celebration and if you want to pray you can pray anywhere you want...in your room, a church, on the stage, wherever you want. And if I want to use the liturgical music for 'The Hands', I use it. I am sorry if I offend, but I will continue to use it. I chose the music because the Russian Orthodox music has such a capacity for sufferance. It is different from the Gregorian chant which is (he gestured and sang the airy, floating chant) so ethereal, without body. It is cool passion. There is no sufferance. The Russian chant is real, coming from the soul. There is a big difference and this is why it was very good for 'The Hands.'

Adelaide: "If you did the Passion mime would you use music?"

Marcel: "Oh yes! I would use music, absolutely. I would use all J.S. Bach, but I'm afraid that it has been used too much. You have the beautiful film that Pasolini has done. It was beautiful because it showed peasants playing the Passion. I think that the greatest part of it was the Crucifixion. It was the greatest moment. If I would do it, I would use Russian Orthodox music.

"What is interesting to you about what I do?"

Adelaide: "I've mentioned specifically the three religious mimes, but I think all of your mime expressions have a spiritual or religious quality about them. In 'Contrasts' I was again aware of the Christ figure at the end."

Marcel: "Yes, religious in the sense of love for humanity. It's never putting a man down through laughing. It's always a gentleness in the touch, in the gesture.

"I will tell you something very interesting. I played 'Bip in the Modern and Future Life' one evening in Geneva. After the performance a Jewish professor came to see me. He was a cabalist. (Cabalism is an occult religious philosophy developed by certain Jewish rabbis, based on a mystical interpretation of the Scriptures.) He asked me if I had studied cabal. I said, 'Not at all. I have heard of la Cabal as a science.' 'Because,' he said, 'you have gestures which are religious gestures, which are the cabal.' 'Well,' I said, 'what religion has invented, what Jewish priest or the Catholic priest or the Protestant minister performs, they have all been inspired in the language of sign. Language of religion has been created by man in a religious sense and we all do the same gestures. The New Testament took from the Old Testament some of the signs because men are men. A religious belief is a religious belief, you know.

"In the Buddhist religion, if you look at it in the sense of gesture, Japanese Noh dancing is very religious, because it is Buddhist. And if you look at Buddha, you look at the hands, you see the same attitude that you see in the old Russian churches in the icons. The 12th and 13th century sculptures made hands like this (he gestures the hand blessing, the hand teaching). Why? Because the hand is the most typical expression which is seen and understood by thousands, even at a great distance.

"At the end of 'Contrasts' when the man does this gesture, it's a holy idea of the spirit which will prevail and as long as the Spirit persists, man will not be doomed.

"Also in the 'Creation of the World', if you see what I want to express, when Adam and Eve have been chased from paradise, the key thing for me is that now they begin to work. They will suffer. They will learn that nothing is given, for nature does not give by itself if man does not know how to earn it, through sweat and blood, through love and all that is human. This is the contrast, what the Chinese call the 'yin and yang' of life. If there is light, there is shadow. If there is day, there is night. And maybe, if there would be only love in the world and no contrasts, there would be no death. It would be eternity. On that day there would be no more hate and no more contrasts. Life would be eternal.

"Maybe this happened once, that life was eternal, before man was created. In this sense, maybe we could arrive at this. We do not know yet. We are at the beginning. We are at the beginning of an eternal life. I am very interested in this. I am just now reading Teilhard de Chardin. I'm going through it again. He must have been a very revolutionary person in his time, eh?"

Adelaide: "Have you ever done any of your mimes in a church setting or with a liturgy?"

Marcel: "No, but I am always astonished at the priests and Sisters who come to talk with me, even before I had my religious numbers. Many have written to me, beautiful letters. But I have never worked with the church. I have played in front of churches, in France. It was not specifically religious, but we played in front of churches in the open air. It was beautiful, Marvelous! And I have contact with French priests, mainly because I play in prisons."

Adelaide: "What you do has a deep religious impact. It is celebration of the human spirit."

Marcel: "It is an important thing to bring the arts and religion together. It is a very beautiful thing. It brings life to the world, of course. I am preparing some new numbers now. One is called, 'The Man Who Sold Dreams'. He gives dreams to people and he gives his last dreams to people to help them. He gives everything: you want food, you need money, he gives it; you are old, he gives you youth; you are not loved, he gives you love. He gives everything. And what is left of him? He has only his heart. Suddenly he gives his heart and he has nothing left and then he has only to die, but he will not die, so he becomes a pure spirit and goes through eternity. This I want to create.

The interview ended with the feeling that somehow we had touched a common source. The man, the mime, the clown, the artist of life were one in Marcel. There was a wholeness about him.

Working with MIME

Everyone can benefit from the learning experience of mime. Clergy, teachers, choral directors and anyone who needs to communicate effectively with groups of people can improve their communicative style by studying the meaning of gestures, which is the medium of mime. Please understand that mime is an art that requires great discipline and developed technique. The artist, like Marceau, makes mime appear to be effortless fun with a touch of clowning, or dramatic flourish with the spice of bravado. For the beginner, the art of mime necessitates concentration and the ability to control various parts of the body. The art of illusion depends upon balancing imbalance, that is, achieving the appearance of being acted upon by invisible forces.

Good mime must be believed to be seen. If your art is to be received by a larger group, it must first begin from an inner conviction that what you have to say and the way you choose to say it are important. As a mime, you are giving form and space dimensions to a world of the imagination. This is an involving art for the audience. Each person in the audience will enter into the imaginative world of the mime in a unique way. This requires that the creator must design a mime in such a way that it touches the common experiences of the people.

I have found that mime is highly adaptable to the liturgy. Unlike drama or dance, which usually require a particular setting and space, mime creates the illusion of place and space. In fact, classic mime insists on this artistic simplicity. There are times, however, when the work can be enhanced by such a simple prop as a hat, or a cane, a bench or an umbrella. Mime requires only that the audience have a good vantage point. Outside of that, mime can happen anywhere.

In the next pages, I want to share with you some ideas and exercises which will be useful in developing your own sense of mime and meaningful gesture.

Costuming and Make-Up

Like all clowns, the mime will develop his or her own personal trade-marks of clothing and facial make-up. The white-face, which has become so classic in mime performances, was first developed as a means for increasing the 'universality' of the performer. The mime became a symbol of all people, an 'everyman' to the world. Unlike the masks worn in ancient theater, the white-face allowed for more expressive flexibility.

Your choice of costuming will depend on the kind of character or life situation you want to develop. Baggy pants communicate the bumbling fool, but they also hide effective leg movements. Give careful thought to what your costume communicates.

My costume for 'Curly' was simply light-weight overalls worn over a red leotard top, white-face and a curly wig. The pants material had a pattern reminiscent of the Harlequin's costume, one of the traditional comic characters in pantomime. I selected bright, playful colors that would communicate my own enthusiasm for life. The costuming allowed for freedom of movement as well as Spirit.

The EFFECT of the Cause

We assume that for every effect there must be a cause. This is a basic principle in mime. However, the <u>causes</u> are invisible. It is the reaction, or the <u>effect</u>, that is pantomimed. Reacting effectively is a special discipline, for there is an inner rhythm of timing that must be perfected. Here are some easy studies to work on:

The "CLIC"

This term refers to that instant of release in a movement, an accent which marks the body's passage from immobility to movement to immobility. The 'clic' gives a sharpness to beginnings and to endings. Such punctuation must become part of the mime's movement vocabulary.

For example, touch a clear glass window with your palm. Notice how your hand stops when it makes contact with the glass. And when you remove your hand, you pick it up and place it on another part of the glass. This stopping and starting is the essence of the 'clic'. Now apply this same practice to a mime in which you are inside a glass box. Feel the glass walls. A helpful idea is to use both hands and keep one hand in place on the 'glass' while the other hand moves. This builds the illusion of a stationary wall. Try this in front of a mirror.

The BALANCED Imbalance

Have you ever noticed how a mime artist will create the illusion of leaning on a wall or resting an arm on a fireplace mantle? In order to do this, the mime must develop a sense of balanced imbalance, that is, the ability to maintain equilibrium of the body even when the weight of the body is shifted in such a way that normally a person would fall over or 'lose balance'. Here are a couple of exercises you can try for developing your balance-imbalance sense:

Leaning against the wall - with your arm outstretched towards the side, lean against the imaginary wall. You'll feel the tension in the leg nearest the 'wall'. This is where all the weight of your body is being placed. Try bending your arm and rest upon the 'fireplace mantle'.

Walking into the wind - imagine a strong wind coming at you and try walking into it by leaning forward. Where do you notice your weight falling this time?

Simple Beginnings

In working with mime, as with any other art form, begin with simple ideas and easy exercises. Think of developing a 'mime vocabulary' just as you would develop a speaking vocabulary. Start with simple movements and grow. I have listed some excellent books at the end of this chapter which will provide useful teaching procedures for your work.

For beginnings, try some of these classic mimes:

Walking in place - be aware that when you walk your whole body moves, not just your feet. Study how people move in life. Some people lead with their heads, others with their stomach, while some seem to bounce or toddle. People move fast or slow. Walking in place requires the skill of sliding the heel back towards you, as if you were pulling the sidewalk to you, instead of taking the forward step.

Walking on clouds - try to achieve the lightness of step that would be a
        style of walking on billowy clouds. What would happen if a
        storm came along and blew your clouds away? How would you be
        able to stand up under such a strong wind?

Selling balloons - first you must blow up the balloons and then locate
        yourself in the park where children and adults pass by. Maybe
        some of your customers are so small and lightweight that one
        of the balloons might start to carry them off into space.

Tug of war - this requires that sense of balanced imbalance that I spoke
        of before. Work directly into a mirror so that you can study
        how you can best create the illusion of the pulling struggle
        that goes on in the rope pull. If you are working on a small
        stage with wings on both sides of the stage, you can add a
        comic touch by pulling in one direction and going off stage.
        Then run around behind the stage and re-enter from the other
        side, but this time you are being pulled.

Riding a horse - try this as if the horse were walking, trotting, gallop-
        ing, etc.

Trapped inside a box - using the technique of 'clic' as described earlier,
        imagine that you are inside a box which has four sides, a top
        and a bottom. How did you get in there? How do you get out?
        Use your two hands to define the size of the box. Sometimes,
        with a group, I will invite three or four other people to help
        rescue the person from inside the box.

Catching and throwing a ball - imagine that you have found a very tiny
        ball and that you find it has magical growing powers. Whenever
        you throw it to someone and that person throws it back to you,
        the ball grows in size until it becomes so big that you can't
        throw it any more.

Lifting and holding - use your imagination and lift objects that are of
        different weights and sizes.

A Walk in the park - with this mime you will need to create different illus-
        ions at the same time. For instance, with thumbs locked and hands
        spread, let your fingers flutter like the wings of a bird. You
        see the bird on a branch or on the ground and you move near it.
        It flies wildly away, perhaps to return and perch on your head
        or shoulder. You might introduce yourself to children at play,
        or to people having a tug of war, playing ball. You might take
        over for the balloon man when he goes to lunch. You might have
        to walk against a strong wind. The park walk allows for many
        opportunities to use some of the ideas developed earlier.

After you have become familiar with some of the elements of mime and the possibilities and limitations of your body, then the creating begins. Remember that mime is a total body expression. The importance of facial gestures for communicating feeling will need to be stressed as much as the bodily gestures. Try out your ideas among some friends or with people who have an interest in mime. Creative criticism will be important for growth in this art. Be sure to work on the simplest actions. These often take hours to perfect, but they are the movements most universally understood and appreciated.

Mime and the Liturgy

Because of it's adaptability to the given space and its power to communicate the silent saga of the human situation, the art of mime is effective in the liturgy. It has a proclaiming and prophetic quality. It has the style of the 'nevertheless', that is, when situations pull you down you can still rise up, brush the dust off your pants and try again. A well-designed three minute mime, may be able to say more than a twenty minute sermon.

A mime artist, dressed in white-face and costume, can also get away with much more than the black robed minister. The congregation will anticipate the humor and surprise of someone dressed in white-face. Their corporate imagination is awakened, particularly when the artist is silent. Then, the people must watch what is about to happen and make their own interpretations.

Study the movements of the minister or priest. I would guess that there is already some symbolic gesturing going on in the liturgy. The raising of hands for the benediction blessing is really a symbolic mime which tells a history of heritage. How effective might your worship be if words were minimized and gestures were maximized.

On a number of occasions, we've developed mime pieces for the liturgy, often using the scriptures. For instance, I dressed as Wobbles the clown for a church service at DePauw University. This was on the Sunday before Halloween. The culture of costuming was very much in the minds of the people. I used the 'parable of the sower' for the mime. This was familiar to the congregation. I emerged from behind the pulpit carrying a bag filled with balloons. The balloons were the 'seeds' that I was going to scatter. Some seeds fell on sandy soil and winds blew them away. Some fell among thorns and the thorns strangled them (I used needles to burst the balloons). Some fell on the road and people stepped on them. (People in the congregation stepped on the balloons and broke them). But some seeds fell on good soil and grew many times over (Here I pulled out some balloon animals and flowers and passed them out to the children in the church).

The minister picked up on the imagery of the seeds and built the service around costumes, masks and the clowning spirit. This was very important because so often mime or dance is simply "brought in" and clumsily inserted into a service. In using mime in worship, we need to understand the importance of the art and the symbolic significance of the gesture.

In June, 1973, at the Lutheran Society For Music, Arts and Worship Conference, the Minneapolis Mime Troupe was involved in a liturgy celebrating the event of Pentecost. Following an opening call and response, readings and hymns, a long series of readings were shared by the congregation in an antiphonal style. The readings built upon the following thematic ideas:

CHOSEN (I Peter 2:9; II Tim. 1:7-9); JOINED TOGETHER (Eph. 2:20-22); PROCLAIM (Eph. 6:14-18; Ps. 143:10; Isa. 55:10-11; John 8:31-32); LIVE (Ps. 22:27-28; Rev. 21:3) and THEREFORE GO (Matt. 28:19-20).

A "Response To the Lesson" was created by the mime troupe. It began with a lone figure walking up the aisle of the church, in silence. He waved at the congregation but got no response. He tried several times to get the people to wave back at him. Having no success, he fell asleep at the base of the altar. A sign was held up saying, "YOU ARE CHOSEN". Another mime entered and approached the sleeping figure. He woke the sleeper up to the news that he had been chosen. At first, the mime refused to accept the fact. Soon he began to find others who would help him accept the chosen-ness and try to bring life to the congregation.

The community of mimes proceeded to get all tangled up (JOINED TOGETHER) but realized that they could not move out in the world if they were all knotted up. In the picture below, the mime in black is putting on the armour of God (Eph. 6:14-18) with the help of some of the other members of the troupe. This is the section of PROCLAIMing. A voice from the very back of the congregation shouted: "Now what?" The response was the sign "LIVE". Balloons and confetti streamed down from the balcony as the mimes danced. When the excitement was over and the voice from the back shouted: "Now what?" The response was "Go!" The mimes lead the congregation out of the church building into the street where the closing hymn, "All People That On Earth Do Dwell", was sung in the midst of downtown Minneapolis traffic.

The most intriguing aspect of the mime was the surprise element. The
congregation didn't know ahead of time that the Scripture reading would
receive the silent interpretation of the mime troupe. The moving from
the church building was also an unexpected quality that deepened the
meaning of the words which were read earlier.

Mime with a Twist

When mime is being prepared for use in liturgy, there should be a clear
understanding as to its purpose and style. I feel that it is wrong to
use mime merely as a clever way to illustrate a story or to dress-up
a sermon. It is also a misuse of mime to simply 'plunk' it into a service as if to fill an open slot. Mime takes time to develop a meaning
for the viewer. The mime artist needs time to really transport the
community into the scene in which the action takes place.

Mime is much like a parable — it will have many possible interpretations.
It usually takes something that is very common to daily experience and
helps us to understand ourselves and to see beneath life's surface. Mime
will probe human nature, acknowledging and affirming our basic dignity.

Mime often has a surprise ending — a twist. It is the unexpected conclusion, usually filled with humor and poignancy, that gives mime its
impact. Here is an example of the twist ending as created by mime, Dan
Kamin, a most gifted artist:

> A diver starts out in a rowboat in search of something.
> He looks furtively around to see if anyone is watching
> him. As he nears the right spot, he puts on his diving
> gear and lowers himself into the water.
>
> Deep under water, he is momentarily distracted by the
> various sea creatures passing him. Then he spots the
> sunken treasure. He ties a rope to the trunk handle,
> returns to the surface, climbs into the boat and begins
> to pull. The boat is nearly over-turned by the effort,
> but finally he pulls the treasure into the boat.
>
> He opens the trunk and can hardly contain himself with
> the joy of his newly found wealth. He starts to row
> back to shore. As he rows, it seems as if the boat is
> settling down, yes, it is sinking. Before too long,
> only his head is above water...and the lights dim out.

Dan Kamin

You walk getting nowhere
You walk everywhere that way.
You took the colors from your
    face and put colorless colors
    on your face.
You have no face left
You can have anyone's face.
When you pull at nothing —
    all of you is pulled by it.
You push nothing and everything
    in you is pushed by the
    emptiness which you
    have invented.

— from DAN KAMIN, a poem by Daniel Leger

FURTHER READING

Alberts, David. _Pantomime: Elements and Exercises._ illustrated. 69pp. 1971.
University Press of Kansas, 366 Watson Library, Lawrence, KS 66045.

Kipnis, Claude. _The Mime Book._ Harper & Row, Publishers, New York, 1974.

Explains clearly and in a fascinating way, the theory and technique of
mime. There are excellent photographic illustrations of all techniques
covered. The best source book available so far.

Lawson, Joan. _Mime: The Theory and Practice of Expressive Gesture._ illus.
(paperback) Dance Horizons.

McLelland, Joseph C. _The Clown and the Crocodile._ John Knox Press,
Richmond, VA. 1970. (paperback)

Is life worth celebrating? This small book looks at the role of the
clown and the dance of life through the development of the performing
arts. It delves into the philosophy of clowning.

Mendoza, George. _Marcel Marceau Alphabet Book._ Doubleday, New York, 1970.
Marcel Marceau Counting Book. Doubleday, New York, 1970.

These two delightful picture books were designed for children, but make
excellent studies for a mime group.

A selection of books by Pierre Teilhard de Chardin:

The Divine Milieu: An Essay on the Interior Life; Harper Torchbook TB384,
Harper & Row, New York.

The Future of Man; Harper & Row, New York.

The Phenomenon of Man; Harper & Row, New York.

Building the Earth; Avon Book Division, New York.

Some good resource people include:

T. Daniel, 2326 Greenwood, Wilmette, IL 60091
Dan Kamin, Harlequin Enterprises/604 N. Saint Clair Street,
Pittsburgh, PA 15206

spirit ~ bodied

LITURGY

by REV. KENT E. SCHNEIDER

Kent E. Schneider, jazz musician and composer, is ordained in the United
Church of Christ. His special ministry is in celebration, that is, the
prophetic and proclaiming role of contemporary arts in communal worship
and the life of the community. He has given this work his full-time
commitment for the last seven years. He has traveled throughout this
country and Canada enabling churches to grow in an understanding of the
need for authentic contemporary styles of expression in worship. He
introduced the first use of jazz in a religious service in the United
Church of Christ in 1966. Since then, he has continued to write and
compose new music for the Church. His hymn, "The Church Within Us," is
widely known here and in several foreign countries. Kent's music is sung
and played wherever people are searching for a rhythm that catches the
heart and meaning of today. His music invites dancing.

Kent's early experience with dance goes back to his own backyard in Chicago.
As a young boy, he played trumpet and tap danced at the same time to draw
a crowd for the puppet shows created by his two sisters.

Kent has a special gift, as a leader of worship, to draw people into the
deeper meaning of their own experiences. His latest book, THE CREATIVE
MUSICIAN IN THE CHURCH, is an outstanding contribution to the cause of
religious renewal and musical growth in the Church.

SPIRIT-BODIED LITURGY

by Rev. Kent E. Schneider

> Faith without action is dead...
> and a body without Spirit is lifeless.
>
> James 2:26

We speak of the church as the Body of Christ, a bodily communion of believers who seek to be one with Jesus. To respond to the invitation: "Come, follow me," means to member that Body. Had Jesus been simply a prophet or a good teacher, he would have needed only pupils and listeners. He would not have needed followers. But the Incarnation of God in the form of Jesus the Christ meant that those followers would become incarnated, not only in His teachings, but also in His Body.

In crucifixion and death, Jesus' earthly body was transformed into a new body, a new humanity that went beyond the limits of the flesh and this world. As we member Christ's Body in Baptism, we put on the new Christ nature and put away the old ways. We share in affirming the communion of his Body when we take the wine and bread of the Lord's Supper. We are baptized in Christ (Gal. 3:27, Romans 6:3) into one body (I Cor. 12:13) And within this unity the Lord's Supper sustains us as members. In these symbols, we are in Christ and Christ in us.

With Christ's ascension, the Church became his Body on earth. Constituted by people with varying abilities, vocations, visions and gifts, the Church is ONE in Jesus Christ. This one-bodiedness does not mean that we must all be about the same work in the same way. The Body of Christ is many-membered (I Cor. 12:14). Yet it will be impossible to be part of this communion as an isolated individual. The kind of Christ-body existence I speak of is one in which people feel deeply for one another. Our time together, particularly in worship, is not merely to put in an appearance at some dignified weekend religious ceremony to have _my_ soul up-lifted. Christian existence is a continuing invitation to become personal. Our times together are occasions to be who we are, rather than chances to diffuse off into the anonymity of a group. Christ invites us to take memorable membership in his ministry.

> "Just as the hand must function differently than the foot, so
> each member of the Body of Christ must take on particular
> bodily functions, always realizing that no one part shall do-
> minate if all parts are to serve."
>
> (Rom. 12:5, I Cor. 12:12)

The hand cannot replace the foot; the foot cannot replace the eye. Each member maintains a distinctive identity and purpose in the total work. That identity of the person is possible only in membership of the united body in service.

The Body provides a medium for expression, movement and action. If any body fails to exercise its natural capabilities it will grow weak and soon become lifeless. It becomes clear from Paul's thematic development of the Body of Christ and from our own ability to understand history, that the teachings and life of Jesus were not intended to be turned into programs, policies and positions. If this were true, the Church as Christ's Body, would be quite comfortable simply sitting around conference tables, or in the church pews, talking to one another. Rather, Christ calls each of us to live life in his own style, willing to suffer for others that all might have new life. Without Spirit, courage and conviction our bodies will be dead. Without action to our words, our faith is lifeless. Without direction and momentum, the physical body will wander and lose its way. Without direction of the Spirit, the Body of Christ will travel in self-protecting circles.

God Calls ~ Man Responds

Whenever the Spirit moves, there is an <u>urgency in action.</u> God calls and man responds. Christ invites us to come, and we follow. There is an immediacy to the Spirit-Bodied Christ in us. The Kingdom of God is at hand. The situation is present and we are within it. We cannot postpone or ignore that which is before us. The <u>Way</u> is our life path, the <u>Truth</u> is both the joy and the suffering, and the <u>Life</u> is new existence.

The Spirit-Bodied community exists in <u>honest communication.</u> We make time to interpret the meanings of our shared experiences and to try to get down to the deeper meanings. Without this face-to-face speaking, there is no community, there isn't even much semblance of persons. Each of us exists in a shut-up aloneness, in isolation.

> "I remember times when I've failed to keep up a commitment that I've made. I was afraid to talk with that person, not knowing how angry they might be. I lived with disappointment in myself for having failed to act out what I said I would. My lack of communication only made the hurt grow inside. Finally, realizing that silence wasn't a solution, I talked with that person. Rather than evading it, I dealt with my own failure to follow through. And I found that I was still accepted by that person. A great weight had been lifted from me."

To honestly communicate doesn't always mean that we simply exchange information. Communicating is <u>interchanging persons</u>, exchanging interiorities, and accepting the offering from that other person. It is a communing.

The Spirit-Bodied community is <u>caring and sharing life.</u> There is no need to sit in the balconies of life, being a spectator to what is going on. You are among a community of people who express their concern for your well-being, your health and wholeness. Within this caring, a whole spectrum of feelings become possible. We confess our times of threat, aloneness, confusion. We share our joys, exuberance and spirit.

We realize that in our honesty we may not please everyone, all of the time. But we also know that the community will not "turn its back and walk away." Caring and sharing are gifts and risks for which my life is accepted.

Jesus Christ took our humanity upon himself in his own body. He lived it through, stretching himself to the limits of that humanity. Then he went beyond the confines of death into new life. This new humanity of Christ is offered to us. The Body of Christ, the Church, is the place of this acceptance, the place of peace between God and mankind.

"The peace of Christ —to which you are called in one body."
Col. 3:15

In that Body, God finds each of us and we find our acceptance with God.

The Bodiliness of Liturgy

"...present your bodies as a living sacrifice, holy and acceptable to God, which is your spiritual worship."
Romans 12:1

The early Christian church developed a style of liturgy before it developed a style of theology. Worship was experiential, a living faith. Being a follower of Christ meant that your life was one of participatory offering of your whole self. Being the Body of Christ meant that our physical Presence in the world as the living stones of God's Temple (I Peter 2:5) was our witness to life in Christ.

The early church drew upon the writings and testimonies of those who had been close to Jesus. The liturgy became the embodiment of the beliefs of those who gathered for worship. The Christians borrowed from the culture and the Jewish tradition for their liturgical forms. The incorporation of movement and dance was important to the worshipping community. Documents from the first four centuries indicate that the Christians danced a great deal in places of worship, in the yards and on festival days around the graves of the martyrs.

As the faith grew, so did the critics. Gnostics sought to separate the body from the spirit, the flesh from the soul. The sensuality of the body was deemed unholy. St. Basil the Great, Bishop of Caesarea (A.D. 344-407) registered his shock at seeing a dance at an Easter service:

"Casting aside the yoke of service under Christ...they... shamelessly attract the attention of every man. With unkempt hair, clothed in bodices and hopping about, they dance with lustful eyes and loud laughter; as if seized by a kind of frenzy they excite the lust of the youths. They execute ring-dances in the churches of the Martyrs and at their graves, instead of in the public buildings, transforming the Holy places into the scene of their lewdness. With harlots' songs they pollute the air and sully the degraded earth with their feet in shameful postures."

quoted in E. Louis Backman, Religious Dances in the Christian Church and in Popular Medicine (London: Allen & Unwin, 1952), p. 25.

In the centuries that followed the battle over the body, movement and dance in worship only continued. By 1298 the Council of Würzburg declared that dancing in the church and church yards was a sinful action. By the time of the Reformation "ceremonial action" was being re-evaluated for its meaning in worship. The feelings of the time were characterized by John Calvin's Institutes (1:4:3):

> "Men can do nothing but err when they are guided by their own opinion" and those "who introduce newly invented methods of worshipping God really worship and adore the creation of their own distempered imagination."

quoted from Bard Thompson, <u>Liturgies of The Western Church,</u> p.195

Calvin favored a style of liturgy which would be rigidly followed so as to end "the capricious giddiness and levity of such as effect innovations." Only those actions which made for order, decency and reverence could be used. The use of external forms was a distraction from the spiritual worship of God. Calvin argued that "external worship is an evasion; by performing all manner of ceremonial 'subterfuges', men really hope to escape the need of giving themselves to God." He insisted that the Incarnation was meant to deliver the people from the symbols of the old worship and that a reversion to the ceremonies would serve no other end than to "obscure the clarity of the Gospel." He reasoned that those churches that clamor for bric-a-brac suffer from a lack of sound preaching. Idols arise when preaching declines in his opinion.

Another reformer, John Knox, in his <u>Forms of Prayers</u> (1556) specifies that even when the bread and wine are being passed that scriptures should be read so that "our eyes and senses may not onely be occupiede in these outwarde signes of bread and wyne, which are called the visible woorde: but that our hartes and myndes also may be fully fixed in the contemplation of the lordes death." (Quoted from Thompson, p. 304).

With the growing availability of printed Bibles and printed books, the action and gestures of the liturgy were replaced by words. As the vernacular replaced the Latin language, many of the liturgical gestures no longer seemed necessary. When accompanied by words, the movements seemed redundant.

The church moved away from the oral-aural tradition of religion into a manuscript culture. Story-telling was replaced by signal-calling. What was central to the ritual was printed and read ——creeds, faith statements, confessions, corporate prayers, scripture readings, hymns and words. Learning the religious language became a case of memorization. Reading had replaced first-hand experience. Repeatability and reduplication became desirable characteristics.

Liturgy developed its own peculiar language which was considered 'sacred' as opposed to the 'profane' words of the culture. An exaggerated sense of what was 'profane' and what was 'sacred' imposed unnatural restrictions on the forms which the liturgy might take. The church became self-protective and judged the worldliness of dance, music, and other arts as far too stimulating to be considered decent for worship. The church, once an over-arching influence on culture, withdrew into a convenient compartment of man's life which was being shaped by growing industrialism and later, technology.

The tyranny of words and printed worship orders, combined with the mis-
trust of the imaginative and the fear of feelings, led to the gradual
suppression of the arts and the spontaneity in the liturgy. Liturgy
became lethargy. The Body became dull, sluggish and uninvolved. Worship lost its event-fullness. We looked to the future through rear-view
mirrors and saw only the past. We became spectators on a service that
was a one-way verbal experience. The only distinguishing marks of the
church were the sacraments properly administered and the Word of the
past, properly preached. Liturgy no longer spoke to the whole body.
It appealed to the eye for attention. We had lost a sense of balance.

The separation of liturgy from life was an unfortunate development. In
trying to rid the worship of the Church of the worldly expressions, the
arts and honest feelings, the liturgy took on a paralyzing stability that
stunted the growth of authentic renewal. Worship was no longer responsive
to the needs of the people, it had become preoccupied with itself. Re-
visioning of the liturgy became obvious when the people were being cut
off from the world. The special forms, the symbols which lack meaning,
the guarded 'sacred', developed into alienation which only contributed
in separating liturgical life from everyday life.

For the most part, reforming the worship of the churches has meant changing
the words. This has resulted in various denominational committees doing
verbal combat over the place of a comma in a creed, slugging it out over
the sexist versus non-sexist language in the hymns and prayers, and the
development of paste-and-scissors compromises which assemble the broken
scraps of various layers of man's history only to end up with an exceed-
ingly dull, characterless imitation of the Lord's Supper. Spirited
liturgy will not happen simply by sticking a jazz group or folk group
into the slots where the organ used to play. Spirited liturgy will not
happen by introducing a dance choir to illustrate the words of the Lord's
Prayer. We cannot put new wine in the old wineskins.

We must move beyond the church of the manuscript culture, beyond the service of the hymn-sandwich, beyond the smorgasbord liturgy where we try to
provide tid-bits that will please everyone. We must move from the idea
that worship is merely ordering of segments (call to worship, confession,
scripture, sermon, prayers, offering, benediction) and re-vision the
possibility of freeing the Body of Christ in a service that expresses the
wholeness of life and the holiness of living. Liturgy is to be the dependable expression of a people's beliefs in significant symbols that provide fresh awakenings to God's Presence.

I think it will be helpful to distinguish between the qualities of the
liturgy of the manuscript culture and the liturgy of the Body of Christ.

Liturgy of the Manuscript Culture	Liturgy of the Body of Christ.
God is known for past events. God is unchanging, the same. God is stability in a moving world.	God is known in the present as well as the past. God is anticipated in the future. God is creating, always new, ever-coming.

Liturgy of the Manuscript Culture

Christ is the sacrificial lamb whose death atones for our sins. Christ must be protected from an ungodly world.

Liturgy is fixed, a repeatable commodity. The individual always knows what is coming next. There is no need for spontaneity. Nothing unexpected happens.

The minister's job is to lead us in worship. The congregation is preached at, sung to and prayed for. Spectating is a way of life. Monologue is the style of speech.

The liturgy is printed and read. The eye dominates the senses. The service is one-way verbalisms by the minister. Everything is proper, polite, in 'good taste' and reverent.

Liturgy gives us rules that show us what we should not do in the world. Liturgy is restriction from. The Ten Commandments tell me "You shall not...."

Worship is personal between me and God. I am a sinner in need of forgiveness. I look forward to salvation in the Kingdom.

Forgiveness of sins is a weekly aspirin of words that the clergy speaks. It will be repeated next week also.

The service is sermon-centered. Sermons are built upon quotes from the latest books or what others have said. If you miss a service you ask, "What did he say?"

Liturgy of the Body of Christ

Christ chose to suffer to redeem God's people. Christ is in the midst of the world, among the people.

Liturgy is a dependable expression of a people's beliefs. It is a natural characteristic of their feelings for God. It is fresh and originating, open to the Spirit.

The liturgy is the expression of those who gather. The congregation assists in forming prayers, sharing songs and shaping the dialogue. Participating is a way of life.

The liturgy is experiential. Print is minimal. Face-to-face communication is prevalent with opportunity for members to speak, pray, sing and dance. The wholeness of the person is present.

Liturgy offers direction to make us freedom for acting in the world. The Ten Commandments tell me "You are free not to...."

Worship is communal as well as personalizing. I seek forgiveness from God and also from those members of the community that I have hurt. The work of the Body of Christ is here in the world, not in some eternity.

Forgiveness is an action done by Christ for creation. We are asked to forgive one another constantly.

The service is centered in the action of the bread breaking, a significant community symbol of the Body. The sermon grows from first-hand experience. If you miss a service you ask, "What happened?"

Liturgy of the Manuscript Culture

Worship dwells in the past when God acted. Nostalgia characterizes our thoughts of the past - which was better than what we have now. A fixed liturgy enshells the people in the past making them fear the present, alienated from the meaning of the moment.

Worship is a means of being socially accepted.

There is an automatic quality to the liturgy that lets it forge forward at a specified amount of time. There is a deadline to be met. The congregation is that anonymous crowd that punches in and punches out.

The service is ordered in segments: it has a start-stop, start again quality. Nothing ever gets off the ground.

Many symbols, ideas and images compete for supremacy in the service. Sermon, scripture, anthem, hymns and printed pages all express different ideas. Nothing comes through with intensity or clarity.

The language is commanding rhetoric: "Rejoice! Celebrate Life!" or it is signal-calling: "Turn to page #342, stand and sing the hymn." The liturgy is littered with instructions rather than inspirations. Be aware of the *

The Gospel is read, listened to and preached about. Christ is kept in the pages of the printed Book.

The offering is the time when our money is collected by the ushers. It is routine and orderly. The money is sealed in envelopes which have been printed with our names on them.

Liturgy of the Body of Christ

Worship has a sense of immediacy and the meaning of the moment. We understand the past as that which has brought us to the present. We live with a sense of making and shaping history and moving into a future with hope.

Worship is a depth entering into with God and mankind.

We experience the reality of life, both the joy and the sorrow which is offered to God for transformation. There is a timelessness when our worship is filled with meaning. Flexibility is a key quality.

The service has a style, a flow that gives dramatic energy to our life together.

One idea is developed with depth. The whole service builds around this stating it in various ways. The music, drama, dance, speaking words are integrated into the wholeness. There are no dangling ends.

The language is vivid, imaginative and invitational. Worn out phrases, clichés and slogans of the past or the passing-pop are not used for communicating the reality of existence in the Body.

The Gospel is a way of life, a call to action. Without action the Word is disembodied.

The offering is a time of moving, a sacred pilgrimage to the place of offering all that we are. It may take forms of music, banners, poems, dance, as well as money. It is a time of creating.

The manuscript culture values precision, measurement, logic, longevity and repeatability. It dislikes the unexplainable, the abstract, the intangible and the passing. Being dominated by the eye, people of a manuscript culture prefer to keep things at a distance, including one another. The eye is quickly irritated with movement that comes to close. The eye sense also perceives life much better in a sequential pattern. It becomes uneasy when many visual sensations bombard it.

The liturgy of the Body of Christ values the unrepeatable nature of each person in God's creation, the uniqueness and temporary-ness of the gifts that every member brings. The arts of dance and creative music are valued precisely because they speak with an immediacy, a close-ness. They are the momentary witness to God's Spiritual Presence, which is truly a mystery that goes beyond explaining. But this is the preciousness of these gifts, that we cannot hold onto them, just as we cannot hold on to life. The important quality is not to try to hold on, but to fill life with meaning at all times.

It is an unnatural act to try to fit creative dance or creative music into a liturgy of the manuscript culture, precisely because the liturgy of the printed page demands that all action, all life, all bodily Spiritedness, be explainable, logical, evaluated and possessable. Fortunately, the creative artist usually has enough strength and inner conviction to overcome the life-less liturgy of the printed page. Fearing such honest stimulation and expression, such affirmations of creation are labeled 'performances', 'shows' or 'sacrilegious'.

> I attended a worship service which included improvisational music and dance. The musicians played from a lead sheet and then created the melodies as they wished. Their playing and presence was a stirring witness to God's continuing creation in the world. The minister entered in black-robed tradition, read the greeting as it was printed in the bulletin and never left the frozen lines of the printed page for the rest of the service. His sermon, which was read to us from the pulpit, was decidedly lacking in any first-hand immediacy. When the dancers entered as part of the offering, they embodied the exuberance of festivity. They symbolized the wholeness of life which was the appropriate offering for that time and place. The musicians caught their Spirit and continued the creative conversation. The minister returned to read a pre-planned prayer. His life-less tones brought the reality of what was happening back into a deadening past that was no longer available to any of us.

When you are preparing for liturgy, avoid putting the service together in bits and pieces. In other words, don't just take a "call to worship" from one source, a "confession" from another, and a prayer from still another, and stick them together. Avoid using the arts in this same kind of scrap-book way. The expressive arts must flow throughout the service and not just be stuck in the slot where the choir's anthem used to be. It will not work!

Effective liturgy is <u>experiential</u> and has <u>immediacy</u> of meaning.

> We begin by probing "What are the needs, life-experiences and meanings of our people? Where is God moving among the people?

> Don't begin by selecting a theme. This is characteristic of the manuscript culture. By doing this we make the experience fit into or illustrate the given theme. Instead, by beginning with the fullness of the experience and then letting the theme emerge from our probing, the theme idea is the kernel of the meaning which our experience has.

Effective liturgy builds upon the <u>history</u>, the <u>tradition</u> and the <u>faith</u> of the people who have experienced the Christian life before us.

> Effective liturgy touches the living roots of the tradition. We determine where people have participated in the joy and suffering of life, the aloneness and the togetherness? Where has God been known in history? With knowledge of the past, we can better understand the present.

Effective liturgy takes significant <u>form</u>, <u>image</u> and <u>memorable symbol</u>.

> Worship has characteristic style which identifies it as the workings of this people. The language is distinctive and appropriate. At times it cajoles or commands, invites and excites. The language, like the people, is alive.

> Symbols are used effectively in the service. There is not an abundance of symbols, so as to appear confusing. Symbols are selectively used. These are the ones which need no verbal interpretation. The symbols participate with an inner intensity, with that which they symbolize. They say more than words could ever say.

Effective liturgy builds upon <u>one idea</u> and states it in various ways.

> Just as a microscope needs to be focused in order for the viewer to see clearly, so the liturgy must focus the participants so that they will understand what is going on. It is best to take one idea and develop it with depth and richness. This central idea is woven throughout the service in words, music, song, movement, smell, in the visual and sound environments.

> The problem with so many services is that we try to say something about everything. This kind of bombardment leaves people weary or bored. It is anything but a clarifying experience. Confusion should not be mistaken for mystery.

Effective liturgy is the <u>interweaving art</u> of the people gathered.

Like the movements of a symphony, the liturgy will begin by making a statement, a proclamation. The idea will be developed and re-stated through variations. There will be peaks and valleys and a conclusion. There is a sense of direction, a Journey. Liturgy is not a get-away trip into the past, nor is it a quick cook's tour so that we can say we've been there. Liturgy will have a dramatic sense of history and our movement through it as a whole community. There are no loose ends. Each person is inter-woven into a whole Body.

Effective liturgy will be <u>prepared for</u> not planned.

Let's develop that idea of Journey: when you pack you take along what you anticipate you'll need. You chart the anticipated route, though this is subject to change in case you want to stay longer in one place of interest. You prepare for the movement without fully knowing who you'll meet or what new experiences lie around the corner. This is the spirit of making a Journey.

The same kind of spiritedness applies to liturgy: you prepare what you will need, but you can't fully anticipate who you'll share with, what their needs may be, what gifts they bring, what news will be shared. There is a freshness about what we do, even though we may have acted in this way before.

It is essential to keep in mind that there may be some people for whom this Journey is a brand new excursion into the faith. You will need to help these people prepare for the service by beginning with that which we commonly share, namely life, thanksgiving and spiritedness. Your invitation to these people to come and share in the worship will be important words of welcome. If you hope that the people will participate, particularly in communal dance, be sure that the service design leads into a natural kind of participation. Too often good ideas fall flat because we have failed to prepare the people so that a call to dance is answered with a natural response of movement. Nothing is more out of place than forced joy.

Charting the Action

After you've designed a service, check it over and chart out the movement of it. Determine at what points do the people act, move, sing, speak; at what points are the musicians, dancers, singers, liturgists involved?

The following is a chart of Earth Song, a script for a service which is included in this chapter.

The Liturgical Movement of Earth Song:

Movements	Liturgist	Musician	Dancer	Community	Symbol	Action
Gathering		x	x	x		greetings
Centering	x			x		meditate breathing
Life Is A Circle		x	x		dance	
Calling to Worship	x	x	x	x		call-response
Creation's Story I	x	x	x			story-telling
Creation Hymn		x		x		affirmation
Creation's Story II	x					story-telling
Mark 10:46-52	x		x			story-telling
Meditation	x			x		making the story your own
Confessing the weight of the world	x		x			
the news of this day				x		
silent prayer	x	x	x	x		
Lord's Prayer	x	x	x	x		
Rising a new to the wholeness	x	x	x	x		
Offering Doxology dance	x	x x	x x	x x	gifts bread-wine	
Communion Invitation Song Bread breaking Wine sharing Prayer response Song concludes	x x x x x	x x x	x x x	x x x x x		call-response
Going-Out	x	x	x	x		dance

EARTHSONG

by Rev. Kent E. Schneider

The following script is for community, dancers, liturgists and musicians. It builds upon the continuing creation of life which God's people share in each day. It recognizes the freedom that each person has to participate in the creation or to destroy it. The dancers are the central image for this liturgy, giving form and action to the words, giving movement to the liturgical action and inviting the community to move beyond itself to a greater depth of God.

The Gathering

(As the community gathers, let the dancers serve as greeters. Some of the dancers could be dancing outside the church building, using a reading from the Psalms. Musicians (flute or recorder with guitar and bass) might prelude "Lord of the Dance".)

Music for Centering Thoughts:

(After the morning greeting has been shared with the congregation and announcements made, the liturgist would lead the people in the following centering-down experience:)

"This morning I invite you to share with all of us the joy of moving in God's creation, the sense of using the wholeness of our bodies in living praise. We come to participate in the growing awareness that we are to continue the creative, loving work of God in this world.

"When we were created, the scriptures tell that God breathed Life-Spirit into us. This morning be aware of the Life-Spirit within your own breathing. Close your eyes and listen to your own breathing. (Pause) Become aware of breathing-in and breathing-out. Take in from the world what you need to live. Give back to the world what the world needs to live. (Pause)

"And so the life circle goes on............ (music begins)

(The song, LIFE IS A CIRCLE, from the hymnal COME SHARE THE SPIRIT, or from the Vocal Solo Collection, SONGS OF LOVE, is played by the musicians, combined with dancers and vocalist or choir. One style of choreography is described on page 101. Many groups prefer to design their own dance movements.)

Calling to Worship

(After the music fades, the dancers can sit in a large circle in the front of the community. As the liturgist moves into the middle of the circle, the dancers rise slowly to indicate that the community should stand.)

Liturgist: All of life is a call and response. God calls us into creation. God calls us into life. How we live is our response to God. As we share in this call to worship, let your response be these words: 'God calls me this day', and raise your arms as a sign of your response.

God calls us to life! God calls each of us to move among the creation of this world and bring joy and renewing love. God calls us this day!

Community: God calls me this day.

Liturgist: God calls us to Love, to plunge ourselves into the hurts and the horrors, to give ourselves fully to those who are in need. God calls us to be Present to those who are without Love. God calls us this day!

Community: God calls me this day.

Liturgist: God calls us to dance, to act alive and not dead! He calls us to move out our joy and our sadness and not to be so self-conscious in a world that has weight-watchers. No longer can we afford the wait. We are builders of the Body of Christ. God calls us this day!

Community: God calls me this day.

Liturgist: In him we live, move and have our being. Amen.
(Solo voice or choir sings: "and so the earth song goes on and on" as dancers once again begin to move and indicate that the community can be seated.)

CREATION'S STORY

(The following story would be read aloud by a narrator and danced by the dancers. The music used could be Haydn's Creation, or a record entitled: Environments, the Ultimate Seashore. Make sure that you play the tapes or records through a good sound system. If you are using musicians, use a solo flute, recorder, or voice with guitar with "Lord of the Dance," played softly and slowly.)

God, who is without a beginning or an ending, stepped out of Eternity to shape a world. Out of an Infinite Love, more perfect and encompassing than can be imagined, He raised His arm, thundered the command, and the heavens and the earth burst forth in response to the call. The first day.

The light turned its face from the darkness and bathed God's creation.

Then God whirled the waters below into a ball and divided the heavens from the earth. The second day was the response. Next, God gathered up the waters into patterns, separating the dry land, and called out the growing things. And in response, they grew. It was the third day.

On the following day, to guard and to guide the newly forming world, He flung the lights of the sky into orbit and in the fifth day, God broke the silence with the motion and music of creatures of the sea and the sky. They were made for a perfect world.

Finally, God called forth the beasts of the earth. It was now the middle of the sixth day.

And from His immeasurable Love, God stamped His own Presence. He scooped from the dust of the earth a form in His own Image. And God breathed into that form called 'mankind' the breath of life. He called: "Be prosperous and loving." And mankind has been responding in various ways ever since.

In the hush of the seventh day, God rested to see all that had been called into creation. And all was very good.

Hymn of Creation: "For the Beauty of the Earth"

But as the earth song went on, some of the people, who had shared freely in the creation, wanted more for themselves. Some of them wanted to possess the wisdom of the world; some wanted to possess the world's riches. There were some who wanted to make music and dance; some wanted to be actors and actresses; some wanted to be athletes. There were some who felt that music, dance, drama and athletics had no place in the world. It was now the eighth day of creation and things weren't looking good at all.

God called to the people, but they were so busy with their own things that they didn't have time to listen. God sent signs to the people, but still they wouldn't believe. God sent prophets into the cities but the people laughed at their words.

Again God called to us: this time His Word took flesh and came among the people. As a child named Jesus, He came and grew. Surely by now the people would have learned that they cannot possess the world. This was not what God had given mankind breath for. It was now the ninth day of creation and all was not good.

Scripture Reading: Mark 10:46-52

(The following could be dramatized with dancers.)

Jesus and the disciples were leaving the city of Jericho and were being followed by a great crowd. There, along the road was a blind beggar named Bartimaeus. When the blind man heard that Jesus of Nazareth was passing by, he started to shout: 'Jesus, Son of David, have mercy on me!'

And many scolded him, telling him to be quiet. But Bartimaeus cried
out all the louder: 'Son of David, have mercy on me!'

Jesus stopped and said to the disciples: 'Call him.' And they called
the blind man, saying: 'Take heart, rise, he is calling you.'

And throwing off his coat, he sprang and came to Jesus. Jesus said
to him, 'What do you want me to do for you?'

Bartimaeus said: 'Master, let me receive my sight.'
Jesus said: 'Go your way for your faith has made you well.'
And the man gained his sight and followed Jesus on the road.

A Meditation: HE IS CALLING YOU

The following ideas are for your own mind priming:

Jesus gave us many invitations in his ministry: 'follow me'
(Matt. 4:18); 'come to the marriage' (Matt. 22:4); 'come
to me all who labor, I will give you rest' (Matt. 11:28);
and 'come, inherit the kingdom prepared for you' (Matt:
25:34).

When the invitation comes to us we have a number of choices:

-- we can simply refuse and be too busy to attend, like the
    people who refused the wedding feast (Matt. 22:1-10; Luke
    14:16-24),

-- we can attend the occasion but not participate. I re-
    member my very first grammar school dance: the boys stood
    on one side of the gym and the girls stood on the other
    side. The boys watched the girls dancing with each other.
    It was an awkward time of life. How puzzling it must have
    seemed to the parents when we returned home and they asked,
    "Did you have a good time at the dance? Who did you dance
    with?" They couldn't imagine why I had such a good time
    when I didn't dance, but only talked with the fellows. In
    high school, I realized what I was missing.

-- we can attend the occasion with our own agenda in mind.
    Perhaps we have already convinced ourselves that we weren't
    going to have a good time....so we acted that way.

A Time of Confessing

(The liturgist stands in the midst of the circle of dancers who rise
slowly and begin moving counter-clockwise in a circle as the liturgist
speaks. As the words make reference to carrying the world on one's
back, let the dancers start to slump over, walking slower and slower,
until they gently fall to the floor.)

Liturgist: We've all received the unexpected invitation in life. Sometimes
it's been an invitation to help or an invitation to have a good
time and we haven't been prepared for it. Sometimes we cry out
for help or extend an invitation to another and our cry goes un-
heard or the invitation is refused. These are truly lonely times
in our lives.

At times we live as if we are carrying the weight of the whole world
upon ourselves. Bills are due, opportunities pass us by and life
seems to be breaking up right in front of us. We keep trudging
around and around, never able to break free, never finding anyone
to help support us through such times.

We have been guilty of looking at ourselves.

(At this point readings from the newspaper of the day would be appropriate.
These short readings would come from the community.)

We must rise out of that darkness, that aloneness. Each of us can
respond to God's call. Each of us can get out of that old path
of life and respond to Jesus' invitation to 'Come, follow me'.
Each of us has been called. What is your response this day?

Take a few moments to pray.

(After the time of silent prayer.)

"Come to me, all who are tired from carrying those heavy loads,
and I will give you rest. Take my yoke and put it on you, and
learn of me, because I am gentle and humble in spirit, and you
will find rest. The yoke I will give you is easy, and the load
I will put on you is light."   Matthew 11:28

Lord's Prayer (with the whole community)

(Liturgist moves to each member of the dance group still on the floor.
To each dancer is given one of these invitations. Once given, the dancer
rises and shares an invitation to members of the community.)

Rise, for God has come among us.
Rise, for you are a part of God's Loving creation.
Rise, for Christ has taken your burden upon Himself.
Rise, you are not alone in the world.
Rise, Christ has given you the invitation to follow.
Rise, go and spread the news.
Rise and dance, your past is forgiven.
Rise, today God has made you different.

(You may want to punctuate each 'rising' with the chorus of 'Lord of the Dance' and then move into singing the verses as the dancers share the 'rising words' with the congregation.)

Liturgist: The Lord be with you.
Community: And also with you.
Liturgist: Greet one another in a Spirit of Love and forgiveness.

The Time of Offering

(The dancers, who have moved throughout the community with the peace greeting, now return with the communion offering of bread and wine. The 'bread baskets' or offering plates, would be passed among the community. The offering should be made in such a way that it has a personalizing feeling to it: 'The gift without the giver is empty.' As the gifts are received (which might include poetry, banners, new music, etc.), let the dancers bring the offering to the altar. Teach the community the simple movement to the Doxology (see page 127). Let the entire congregation sing it and dance it, led by the dancers and the choir.)

Liturgist: The God who made the world and everything in it, being Lord of heaven and earth, does not live in shrines made by men, nor is he served by human hands, as though he needed anything, since He gives to all people life and breath. And He made every nation of mankind to live on the face of the earth and to seek God, in the hope that we might feel after him and find him. Yet he is not far from each of us, for (the next words could be moved out by the dancers) in Him we <u>live</u>   and <u>move</u>   and have our <u>being</u>.

Acts 17:24-28

The Act of Communion

Liturgist: (speaking to the dancers)
A feast has been prepared. All is now ready. Go out into this community and bring the people. (Speaking to the congregation) Come to the Lord's Table, the feast of Christ. Come, for you are to inherit the kingdom prepared for you.

Hymn: "This Is Your Table" from COME SHARE THE SPIRIT (1st verse only).

Jesus was recognized by his actions following the resurrection. To the travelers on the Emmaus road and to his disciples on the shore, Jesus was known as he broke bread and shared food with those he loved. He tells those who have followed him throughout the centuries that whenever we gather we should share bread as a sign of his life and Spirit among us. Take and eat, for this is the bread of Life, the sign of the risen Lord!

(As the bread is passed the 2nd verse of "This Is Your Table" is sung. Also, the following scriptural readings may be read as the music continues:

"I am the bread of life; come to me and you shall never hunger; believe on me and you shall never thirst."   John 6:35

"I am the living bread which came down from
heaven; if any person shall eat of this bread,
he shall live for ever." John 6:51)

And in taking the cup, he said that this is the New Covenant
which God makes with his people. The wine is the outpouring
of Christ's Life for all of us. Take the cup and drink.

(As the cup(s) is/are passed, sing the 3rd verse of "This Is
Your Table". The following scriptural readings may be used
as the singing ends and the music continues:

"I will not drink of this fruit of the vine, until
that day when I drink it new with you in my Father's
Kingdom."   Matthew 26:29

"I am the vine and you are the branches: abide with
me and I am in you. Without me you can do nothing."
John 15:5)

(Following the wine, a prayer could be offered. We have used
a simple responsive style of prayer in which the congregation
repeats short phrases after the liturgist. For example:

Lord, you have invited us (community repeats phrase)
Lord, you have called us
to share the feast of new life
to eat the bread
to drink the wine.

Send us into the world,
with renewed Spirit,
with fresh Hope,
with enduring courage,
with creation's Love,
to teach and to learn,
how to dance each day a new.

(The 4th verse of "This Is Your Table" would be shared.)

A Time for Going-Out

(A voice from the balcony or some place off in the distance reads:

"Then I saw a new heaven and a new earth; for the first heaven
and the first earth had passed away, and the sea was no more.
And I saw the holy city, a new Jerusalem, coming down out of
heaven from God, prepared as a bride adorned for her husband;
and I heard a great voice saying: 'Behold the dwelling of God
is with mankind, He will dwell with them and they shall be His
people, and God himself will be with them." Revelation 21: 1

Liturgist: May the Lord of all creation dance within you this day. Amen.

(Choir, musicians and dancers lead the community out singing the chorus
of 'Lord of The Dance')

LIFE IS A CIRCLE

This is a dance design for the song, LIFE IS A CIRCLE, which appears on the following pages. This particular dance scripting originated with a dance choir in Fresno, California in April, 1976. The song should be sung in a moderate waltz tempo. It has been used as the prelude in the celebration design, EARTH SONG. The dance movements are a continuous, pulsing flow of circular forms, which is hard to describe in words.

Introduction: use the four bars before the first ending as an introduction.

Come from the community and form a circle.

"Life is a circle that goes round and round,

Slow circle dance, clockwise.

"Touching the heavens...

Stop circle, take one step forward and sweep arms upward.

"and scraping the ground,

Lower arms and body to the ground.

"An endless beginning,

Twirl hands (like paddle wheels) and let hands pull body up to standing position.

"with push and with pull;

Now standing, push out and pull back with arms.

"darkness, light bringing

Arch arms over head, bending arms, head and back down into the center of the circle.

"each one to the full...ness...of

Slowly move into the circle and back out, holding on each of the three musical holds...a pulsing movement.

"starting all over, beginning anew,

Circle dance clockwise, in merry-go-round effect. Dancers alternate bending knees and rising on toes.

"daylight's just breaking, there're fresh roads to choose,

Keep moving in circle, but stop merry-go-round effect. Dancers raise one arm at a time in a dawning effect.

"with new paths to follow and new friends to make,

Do-si-do movement, with dancers stopping to meet and greet one another. Form partners.

"When circles meet circles
ringing us round,
with echoing touch of creation's
sound, and so the earth song
goes on and on
and so the earth song goes on and on
  (keep repeating until dancers finish.)

Partners form circle dances, enlarging to meet other partners. Keep enlarging until all the dancers are included. Spin off into congregation.

Life Is A Circle

Kent Schneider

Life is a cir - cle that goes round and round,

touch - ing the hea - vens and scrap - ing the ground, an

new paths to fol - low with new friends to make, when

cir - cles meet cir - cles _____ ring - ing us round with

ech - o - ing touch of cre - a - tions sound, and

REPEAT AD LIB. and DIM.

So the earth song goes on, and on and

104

FURTHER READING

Adams, Doug. <u>Congregational Dancing In Christian Worship.</u> The Sharing Company, P.O. Box 190, North Aurora, Illinois, 60542. Revised edition 1976.

Backman, E. Louis. <u>Religious Dances in the Christian Church and in Popular Medicine.</u> Allen and Univen, Ltd. London, 1952.

Cox, Harvey. <u>The Feast of Fools.</u> Harvard University Press, Cambridge, Massachussetts, 1969.

Pieper, Josef. <u>In Tune with the World: A Theory of Festivity.</u> Harcourt, Brace and World, New York, 1963.

Rivers, Clarence Jos. <u>Soulfull Worship.</u> Office for Black Catholics, 734 15th Street, N.W. Suite 906, Washington, D.C., 20005, 1974

Thompson, Bard. <u>Liturgies of the Western Church.</u> Living Age Books, World Publishing Co., New York, 1961.

THE ARTS OF CELEBRATION

<u>DIRECTORY OF ARTISTS AND RELIGIOUS COMMUNITIES</u>, ed. Rev. Kent E. Schneider. The Center For Contemporary Celebration, West Lafayette, Indiana. 1975

Ortegel, Sr. Adelaide, S.P. <u>BANNERS AND SUCH</u>, The Center For Contemporary Celebration, 1971.

Ortegel, Sr. Adelaide, S.P. & Schneider, Rev. Kent E., <u>LIGHT: A LANGUAGE OF CELEBRATION.</u> The Center For Contemporary Celebration, 1973.

Schneider, Rev. Kent E., <u>THE CREATIVE MUSICIAN IN THE CHURCH.</u> The Center For Contemporary Celebration, 1976.

<u>THE DESIGNING LITURGY SERIES</u> is a collection of ten books, each forty pages in length. The books provide in-depth ideas, research and resources for planning such events as Christmas, Thanksgiving, Easter, Lent, Baptism, Communion, Marriages and Funerals. The books are available from The Center.

chapter 7

CREATIVE MOVEMENT
for everyone

Movement as Creative Expression

Movement is a primary form of expression from the earliest days of life. This chapter emphasizes the feeling factor that transforms basic physical movement into creative movement. We are not concerned here with finished performances, but with the process; with the originating of gesture and expression. Each person is encouraged to create his or her own unique way of moving and communicating feeling.

The suggestions and exercises offered are suitable for everyone, regardless of age or grace. They can be used with inter-generational groups as well as with classroom or camp or workshop sessions. I have often had severely handicapped persons participating in my classes. Every group is different. There is a new dynamic with each class. The leader of creative movement must be ready to bring her whole self to each new situation —to share a joy and an enthusiasm so that even the most self-conscious beginner will be drawn into the freedom and spontaneity of the movements. Teacher and students grow together in an understanding of the relationship of bones, muscles and breath that makes up the unity of the body. They also grow in an appreciation and a confidence in the limitless possibilities of the human imagination for creative expression.

The exercises suggested here are meant to spark creations in both teacher and student. They are ideas and starting points. Each expression must be felt and modeled anew with each presentation. Some will be discarded or changed. New ones will be invented.

Goals

There are many worthwhile results to be gained from a good session in creative movement. People feel relaxed, exhilarated, refreshed. They have shared a creative experience with others and therefore know each other in new ways. They gain a fresh understanding of communication. It's good exercise. Creative dance techniques are developed. But the most important result of all will be the sense of wholeness, that feeling of being "at home" in your own body.

It is better to begin the movement explorations without music. Since the goal of creative movement is to help the individual rediscover self by getting back in touch with his own thoughts and feelings, it can be distracting to fill the room with images and moods suggested by the music. Melodies tend to carry the person along, imposing someone else's feelings. A hand drum is useful for setting a rhythm pattern.

It is important that proper clothing be worn for the movement experience. Dance leotards and tights are preferable. An alternative would be loose, stretchable clothing that would allow for freedom of movement with a minimum of bulkiness. Since the primary goal is FEELING AWARENESS, clothes should not restrict total involvement.

The Basic Design of a Class

    I. INTRODUCTORY ACTIVITIES

        Warm-ups, loosen-ups and get-acquainted exercises

    II. MOVEMENT EXPLORATIONS - Individual

        Expressive imaginings, textures of movement

    III. MOVEMENT EXPLORATIONS - in Groups

        Creating movements in responding relationships
            Pairs
            Trios
            Larger Groups

    IV. CREATING MOVEMENT STATEMENTS IN GROUPS

This progression of exercises and problems calls for a two-and-a-half to a three hour class time. A break should be given halfway through the period. Time should be allowed for questions and discussion. With groups of young children, one hour or even less will be sufficient. When a shorter span of time is all that can be given for older groups of people, the third and fourth parts of the class design will have to be abbreviated, but the Introductory Activities and the Movement Explorations should not be hurried.

Dancer in a Workshop in Anderson, Indiana, warm-up with elbow exercises.

I. Introductory Activities

Warm-ups are valuable because such exercise psychologically prepares a person to start moving, increases the blood flow, and stimulates sluggish muscles. When you are working with beginners, it will be necessary to lead them slowly and simply into the stretching and flexing of muscles. Caution is needed to prevent injury. If you do not know the physical limitations of the people in the group, take time to explain that each person is invited to participate at whatever degree of exertion the body will allow. If a movement causes pain or undue strain, it should be modified to meet the particular need.

In working with a new group of people, I try to combine the warm-up exercises with a name-game or some kind of "mixer" that will help people feel at home with each other. A "social warm-up" is as important as the physical warm-up. People need to feel comfortable and unthreatened in order to be themselves.

Example:
> Invite the people to remove their shoes and form a circle. They should leave enough space on either side for free movement. Suggest that they move and jiggle around to shake off whatever weights seem to be hanging on them. Sometimes I ask them to find the way they move in the world this day.
> Next, start a rhythm by snapping fingers. People can still move freely, but they begin to do it in rhythm.
> Then ask them to tell their first name:

> "I'm Mary! X X I'm Tim! X X I'm Virginia! X X I'm Bob!"
> 1 - 2, 1-2, 1 - 2, 1-2, 1 - 2, 1-2, 1 - 2.

Continue the sequence around the circle. Usually someone will add a new twist or skip a beat. This gives everyone a chance to laugh, which is the best "warmer-upper" of all. If people can laugh together, they can develop some intensity of meaning together.

Continue the WARM-UP EXERCISES with:

> Roll head in a circle to warm neck area and relax tensions
> Circle the shoulders in a figure 8 pattern
> Circle the elbows
> Stretch the arms and torso upward, forward, sideward
> Roll the foot and ankle
> Roll the hips
> Collapse forward like a rag doll with arms dangling

> Sit down in a comfortable centered position.
> Close your eyes.
> Take time to find your center of being. (See CENTERING EXERCISE
> page 27)

There should be something of an ebb and flow to the energy levels used in these opening experiences. Pace the alternations of exertion and relaxation. The CENTERING EXERCISE is a key to helping the people internalize what they are feeling with their outer senses.

II. Movement Explorations ~ Individual

Begin this section by asking everyone to stand up and walk around the space in a natural way. Eyes should be open enough to see where you are going, but think and feel within yourself.

Continue the experiencing by saying:

> Try walking in a "centered" way. Feel as if the main axis of your body is perpendicular to the floor. This does not mean that you should walk stiffly, but poised and balanced. (Give the people enough time to feel this walking in balance.)

> Freeze. (This is a good direction to use when you wish to change sensings. The people need a neutral time in order to get into the next feeling.

> Let's step into a pool of Jello. First, it is just up to your knees. Try walking through it. Now it is up to your waist. As you move, it gets deeper and is soon up to your neck. Feel it against every part of your body.

> Jump out of the Jello pool and walk naturally again.

> Try the "centered" walk, this time imagining a golden thread tied to the very top of your head. You are being pulled up by this thread, like a puppet on a string. Feel the buoyancy of your body grow with each breath you take.

> Now, imagine that the thread is cut. Your body is growing heavier and heavier. Feel the pull of gravity. Your feet are so heavy that you can hardly lift them. You are getting heavier and heavier.

> Freeze. Take a minute to be aware of how you feel.

> Start breathing in larger amounts of air. Let the air fill you and lift you. Imagine that it is helium and you are growing lighter and lighter. Start walking around. You can hardly stay on the ground. You practically float.

> Freeze. How do you feel now?

Another type of opening exploration is to ask everyone to lie down on the floor. Help them to relax every part of their bodies —to sink down into the primordial ooze. Let them remain that way for a few moments and then suggest the forces of energy gathering to bring about the emergence of life. Perhaps they are clay beginning to be moved and formed. Explore the air, the space above you. Let yourself take form, slowly, individually. This can be a very personal kind of birth or evolution. This whole sequence can be done with eyes closed.

FURTHER IMAGINING WALKS

Move as if you were made of:

smoke	water
fire	glue
clay	wire
mechanical parts	feathers

Besides WALKING, all of these imaginings can be done with movements of SLIDING, JUMPING and TURNING.

Remember, the whole purpose is FEELING, not how you might look.

FREE-FORM MOVEMENT EXPLORATIONS

Another way to explore movement textures is to express in any way you choose, some of the following:

scratchy	red	cold
bubbly	blue	hot
rubbery	yellow	angry
fluffy	purple	smiling
sticky	green	jealous
	pink	free

Choose a machine and create its movements and sound.

III. Movement Explorations in Groups — Creating Movements in Responding Relationships

The progression in this section is from individual, personal explorations to partner and group improvisations. An improvisation is a continuous spontaneous creation of letting one movement flow into the next; not planning ahead, but allowing the immediate action and relationship to call forth a responsive movement. Creative movement is improvisation.

Another important step in this section is the development of the idea of performance as sharing; as the giving of a unique gift. The role of the viewer becomes that of receiver of a gift. This style of sharing makes for a more open and sincere atmosphere. Constructive criticism takes on a more friendly and positive aspect. Nothing is more devastating to beginning creators, people who are risking for the first time, than laughter at the wrong time. I have found that it is good for people to laugh together, to have an opportunity to do hilarious things where the laughter is a part of the group experience. I have also found that it is necessary to form an environment of acceptance and trust if creativity is to be nurtured beyond the first awkward beginnings.

IN PAIRS

Ask the people to turn and quickly find a partner... the person nearest to them. Have them create a HAND DANCE in relation to the movements of their partner; not touching, but using the space cooperatively.

When everyone seems to have mastered the technique, say:

"Freeze. Thank your partner and turn to the person behind you. Begin again with your new partner."

This exercise can be done with 2 or 3 changes of partner. Then ask the people if they noticed that their style of moving changed with each partner. What else happened? Take a minute to discuss the experience.

IN TRIOS

Now have the people form groups of three. Begin in the same way, designing
your movements to relate to the person on either side of you.

You can have the groups change to foot movements or hand and body movements.
A drum beat rhythm can add another variation. Keep the activity fresh and
challenging. Don't let it get bogged down with too much sameness.

Experiment with four or five in a group. Notice how demanding it becomes as
you try to relate your movements cooperatively with the larger grouping.

At various times during this exercise, you may want to ask the group on one
side of the room to pause and watch the other half. This gives everyone a
chance to ease into the sharing later on.

IV. Creating Movement Statements in Groups

Problem I.

To change the mood, ask each group of five to move as if they were machine
parts made of steel. Let them experiment with this for a few minutes, then
suggest that each group find a corner or separate space and create a machine
together. These inventions will then be shared with the whole group one at a
time. It should take only five or ten minutes to prepare the group movement.
Since it is fun and rather comical, everyone enters in whole-heartedly.

Before the sharing, explain that a dance statement should be framed in
motionlessness. The group begins with stillness, creates the movement and

then ends in stillness. As these first creations are shared by a group, let the others guess what machine they are supposed to be, but also highlight the interesting kinds of movement and shapes in space that can be seen.

Problem II.

Have everyone stand up and move around. If the group is large, they may have been sitting for quite a long time. Muscles need to be warmed up again. Have the people choose a new partner for this activity.

In two's, create a pose, something like two sculpture figures that relate to each other in an interesting use of space. Try to use different levels. Create a second pose, remembering the first pose.
Now, see if you can move easily and continuously from the first pose to the second pose. Let the partners work on this problem for awhile. Then call the whole group together and let each pair do their movement phrase for the rest of the group. Usually the sequence is so short that it can be done twice. This will give everyone a better opportunity to see the shape of the movement. Some groups become quite interested in discussing the wider meanings that a series of movements communicate.

Problem III.

Form cluster groups of five. Create a movement design that has three parts:

1. the group is bound or held together in some way
2. something forces or tears them apart
3. something draws them back together

This simple basic movement can take many styles. The group may start in a circle, a line, or a pile. They may think of themselves as an organic whole, or as separate parts. Each group should have a space to work in which will give them enough room and a certain amount of privacy. Twenty minutes is enough time for most groups.

The sharing this time takes on added anticipation. By now the whole group has a keener awareness of the language of movement and of the creative process. The discussion of each movement sharing will expand its meaning and value.

Problem IV.

Another type of Problem along the same line would be:

1. the group is searching for something
2. they make a discovery
3. they react or move in a new way as a result of the discovery

Problem V.

This last Problem makes a leap in another direction. All the previous activity grew from the movement. If meaning was discovered or communicated, it was drawn from the movement itself and our natural understanding of body language and gesture. As a final experience, ask the groups to divide into new clusters of eight to ten people. Each cluster is to go off and design a movement statement that answers the question: "If the whole world would stop and watch you for three minutes, what would you like to say?" People may look a bit floored as they puzzle over the problem, but most groups come up with some powerful non-verbal statements which become quite memorable. They will need at least a half hour to accomplish the task.

Children and Creative Movement

When working with children in CREATIVE MOVEMENT, it is important to remember that they are often just as inhibited as older persons. The self-consciousness reveals itself in different ways with different age groups. In order to draw the children into the imaginative and feeling activities of free movement, you really need to know something about their interests and manners of relating to each other. Listen to them. Try to pick up on some of the things that make them laugh. They have boundless energy and enthusiasm once you get them started.

The girls pictured above were in a workshop in Midland, Texas. They had a marvelous time choosing a favorite animal, individually trying to move and feel the way their animal would move and feel, and then trying to relate the animal they had become to the other creatures in the room. At first this was done in silence, then they added the sounds their animal would make. With this group of young people, it was just the right activity for the time. At another time, or with a group a few years older, it might not work at all.

In working with high school students, I've found that the action must be fast and full of surprising changes. We do a lot of things with an imaginary ball of energy. It can be thrown around the circle like a basketball. It can become the size of a ping-pong ball and worked with in pairs. Sometimes actual props help to free people for creative imagining and moving. A trunk full of old clothes, flashlights in a darkened room, canes, balloons and other such items can become vehicles for expression. Fluid light environments, as pictured on the next page, are another exciting possibility for opening the imagination.

FURTHER READING

De Sola, Carla. <u>Learning Through Movement.</u> Paulist Press, New York, 1974.

A handbook for the teaching of dance as a self-discovery exercise.

Mettler, Barbara. <u>Materials of Dance as a Creative Art Activity.</u> Mettler Studios, Tucson, Arizona, 1960. 418 pages.

A wealth of ideas, exercises and teaching designs for creatively teaching movement expression to large groups. There is a progression of development, so that the book could be used for several years.

Wiener, Jack & Lidstone, John. <u>Creative Movement for Children: A Dance Program for the Classroom.</u> Van Nostrand Reinhold Company, New York, 1969.

This book combines beautifully photographed creative movement experiences with children and a clear explanation of a program that is practical and challenging.

A pair of dancers create a visual statement within a projected light environment. Colored light and slides can add a further dimension to movement improvisations and expand imagination. Techniques for the creative use of projected light are detailed in <u>Light: A Language of Celebration</u> by Kent Schneider and Sister Adelaide Ortegel, published by THE CENTER FOR CONTEMPORARY CELEBRATION.

Christ Takes Form

Kent Schneider

From the hymnal, COME SHARE THE SPIRIT.
Copyright © 1975, The Center For Contemporary Celebration.

CHRIST TAKES FORM is most effective when used as a benediction at the end of a celebration. The picture on the next page shows a group singing it for the close of a winter camp weekend. It is contagious enough that people will continue singing it out into the world. The basic rhythm of it seems to draw people into dancing or swaying it.

Here's how to teach it:

> Teach the bass-tenor line first.
> Add the alto-soprano line next.
> String or electric bass doubles the men's voices.
> Guitars or piano chords gradually pick up the tempo.

The chant-song can be softened to a whisper or a hum while communal prayers are spoken. Have the instrumental group or the accompanist bring the song back in as an affirmation. Sometimes clapping can be added, or small circles can open to form one large circle. This is a song that allows for a variety of responses.

chapter 8

MOVING TOGETHER
congregational possibilities

Congregational Movement Possibilities

Moving together, like singing together, has the power to bring us to a greater sense of community, to make us present to one another in a singularly different way. It breaks down that outer reserve, that mask of privacy that so many of us wear, especially in a group. It frees us to find the simplicity and openness —the child in each of us. This does not mean that we lose our identity in the group action; but that we, in our uniqueness, contribute to a communal spirit. We allow the social sophistication to fall away and we come closer to the truth that is in the human heart. In some cases, our masks for church are the thickest and heaviest of all. It usually takes special motivation and some kind of awakening of the spirit to open us to ourselves.

If the idea of congregational involvement in dance sounds desirable but impossible to achieve, just take a closer look at the movements and gestures we already use in church. These will vary depending upon the type of liturgy, but the standing together, the handshake greetings, the hands raised in blessing, the folded hands, the processing, all of these are forms of expressive movement. Singing together involves some kind of shared rhythmic experience. A Gesture Prayer simply expands upon elements which are already present. If dancing is ever to be a real part of contemporary worship, the whole gathered community must be able to share the experience. Everyone needs to feel the movement and the rhythm in their own bodies. Some people can do this vicariously if they have experienced dance at some time in their lives. But how much more meaningful it can become if they have an opportunity to actually move out their feelings of praise and thanksgiving. Dance is not just for a small group of gracefully coordinated people. It is for everyone.

Leadership

The key ingredient for congregational participation in movement is LEADERSHIP. It is essential to carefully plan the way a community is introduced to the idea of movement prayer. It takes a special kind of sensitivity and enthusiasm to lead communal movement or dance.

PREPARATION

The way the service is designed should prepare the people to want to enter in to the movement, so that the gestures will be honest expressions for them, rather than mechanical or awkward-feeling imitations.

The LEADER should be completely familiar and "at home" with the movements that are going to be used. Church pews naturally limit the scope of movement possible. Get the feel of the movement yourself by trying it in the pews or other space to be used by the congregation.

INVITATION QUALITY

The manner of drawing people into the congregational moving will make all the difference. Invite the people to participate at whatever level will be comfortable for them. Make it easy for people

120

to feel a part of the experience, whether they do it with wide gestures, small ones, or none at all.

If the leader is apologetic or hesitant about introducing the movement, the people will be three times as hesitant and self-conscious.

Project a feeling of sincere enthusiasm and delight and the people will respond with amazing good will.

On the other hand, too much high pressure direction will make the people resent being pushed into it. Avoid anything that might make the experience feel like callisthenics or military drill.

Verbal directions should be kept as simple and brief as possible. The gestures can be learned by imitation. The need is for the people to understand the meaning or meanings of the movements. It is only when the gestures are related to feelings that the people can make them their own. The introduction can take on the meditative style of a Call to Awareness.

Don't worry about those who feel that they aren't ready to try it. Maybe they are actually more involved than you think. The man with folded arms may try it next time. It takes time for some people to find the freedom which is within each of us. Be patient. Be enthusiastic. Most of all, emphasize the point that dance or movement prayer <u>must come from within.</u> It is to be your own individual expression within the group experience of the community. Synchronized, precise movement is not the goal. As in congregational singing, full-bodied honest feeling and a lifting of spirits, is more important.

SIMPLICITY

Use short, simple forms the first few times movement prayers are attempted. Lengthy explanations and rehearsals will bore even your most eager enthusiasts. The words or songs should be already known or easily memorized. You can't do expressive movement with a bulletin or book in hand. The movement itself should be designed with the given environment in mind. Benches and pews require one type of body movement; an outdoor setting calls for another. The leader will need to be adaptable.

DANCERS AS LEADERS

Sometimes it is possible to teach a movement prayer to a small group or dance choir first, so that they can then become catalysts for the larger group. It works well to have the dance choir do the movement sequence early in the service and then have the congregation join with them on a second time or a chorus. It is a good idea to repeat a gesture two or three times during the course of the service. It will begin to feel more natural for the people. When the congregation is more familiar with the basic movement, the dance choir can expand the beauty of the movement just as a singing choir expands the richness of congregational singing.

THE ENDING OR BRIDGE

The ENDING is as important as the BEGINNING of a movement sequence. Plan out how you would like the feeling of the expressive openness to link and carry over into the next part of the service. Sometimes the mood at the end is one of quiet joy and reverence. A moment or two of silence may be appropriate so that people can be still and able to absorb what they have felt. Sometimes a gesture ends in a strong communal affirmation. An immediate swelling response by the full choir might reinforce and expand the feeling. Sometimes the liturgical leader can pick up on the last phrase and develop it into another form of communal prayer. It is most important not to let the ending dwindle into an embarrassed "limbo" time that negates the enthusiasm of the movement.

In the following pages you will find Movement Gestures, Prayers and Songs that I have designed and used while working with congregations in communal celebration. I change and adapt the ideas to meet individual needs, and so should you. As a leader of congregational movement it is vital to develop a wide variety of expressions. Frequent repetition of the same song or movement leads to familiarity and then dullsville or worse.

Amen

This word is a personal affirmation. Invite the congregation to take a stand and speak the word with arms raised. A triple "Amen" with increasing volume provides more time for the people to get into the feeling with some strength.

Alleluia

As a spoken response, this word, which means, "All praise to the Lord most high!" usually sounds pitifully weak. By adding some appropriate arm movements, created on the spot or planned ahead of time, the people can feel the power and joy of the word. The triple ALLELUIA should raise the roof.

Tau Cross

The early Christians, following the tradition of the Eastern world, prayed with arms raised, palms open to the heavens. As a sign of their acceptance of the cross of Christ and the possibility of dying as He did, they extended their arms in the form of the cross. You might invite people to say the Lord's Prayer in this manner. At the end it is a very natural movement for people to reach over and clasp their neighbors hands on the closing phrase. Prayers in the litany form or the "call and response" form are also suitable for the Tau Cross gesture.

Standing

We usually take STANDING for granted, something you must do in order to move somewhere else. That is exactly what it is —a preparation for action. We stand for someone or for some idea. The custom of standing for the reading of the Gospel signifies just that. Ask yourself or your community if sitting is the predominant position in your church.

Processions

The basic symbol, that is, the religious expression of PROCESSING
is one of PILGRIMAGE...a people moving together in a common belief
or cause, to a holy place.

Looking at the Old Testament tradition of Processions we see how
important they were in the worship of Yahweh. Psalm 68 describes
the order:

> "God, your procession can be seen,
> my God's, my king's procession to the sanctuary,
> with cantors marching in front,
> musicians behind, and between them
> maidens playing tambourines."   Ps. 68, v.24,25

In the Early Christian Church, when the faithful were allowed to
worship publicly without persecution, they sang and processed to
the place of worship. Along the way, they would gather newcomers,
inviting them to join the community. It was a literal response to
the Lord's words:

> "Go out into the streets and by-ways and bid them come in."

At the time of OFFERING they brought their gifts of food and clothing,
whatever they had, and placed them around the altar. These gifts were
later shared with the poor in the community.

The GOING-OUT was a re-affirmation of their allegiance to Christ and
their need for help from each other in facing a world of disparate
and opposing values.

A PROCESSION, then, is more than pageantry. It is more than a parade.
It is an embodiment of the spirit of the community on-the-move. It
is a profession of faith...a witness to a living Church. We are the
Church. A PROCESSION is an invitation to enter in and become more
intensely a part of the liturgical experience.

PROCESSIONS require careful organizational leadership. A well-ordered
procession gives people the freedom to enter in without threat of confusion or awkwardness. A procession may be solemn or joyful, but the
singing is an integral part of it.

We process in. We also process out...out into the wider community
to offer service. Sometimes it may be appropriate to use a rhythmic
step as the line moves forward. This is especially effective with a
choir entrance or if the choir is leading the procession. The Afro-
walk step (step with RIGHT foot, bring LEFT foot up and press with a
pulsing, step with the LEFT foot, bring RIGHT foot up and press with
a pulsing, and continue the pattern. This is combined with a clap on
the 2 and the 4 count) can be used, or the Byzantine step (2 steps
forward and 1 step back). The Tripudium (with 3 steps forward and
1 step back) adds more solemnity to the procession. The creative use
of choirs and congregation offers a new dimension in sound and movement. The choir might move as it sings the verses, then pause while
the congregation answers with the chorus. Take a look at your own
church space for processional design.

Besides entrances, PROCESSIONS can be used for:

> the Confession
> the Lord's Prayer or Creed
> the Offertory - Doxology
> the Communion

Invite the people to come up and bring their offering to the altar. Have them gather in a circle or several circles around the altar. The Doxology with gestures (as shown on the next page) works well in this context. Another style might be to have everyone sing the Doxology as if they were standing on the moon looking back at earth. Sustain the endings to add that quality of awe and wonder. Suggest that the people breathe the song as they sing it. It is a beautiful effect, especially in the round. The Communion can be shared in this same circle. People can then return to their original places.

POINTS TO REMEMBER: The PROCESSION should be clearly and carefully planned.
> How will it begin?
> How will it end?

The song or songs chosen should be familiar or easily singable so that people can join in with a full sound. It is harder to sing when walking in a long line.

The PROCESSION should have meaning for the people involved. This requires enthusiastic introduction and motivation.

Open Hands

As mentioned earlier in the book, the gesture of hands clasped tightly has become the most customary position for prayer, at least in the Western hemisphere. But it is not the only way to pray. You might suggest that people open their hands and pray or meditate with palms upward. The hands can rest on the knees or they can be raised to a comfortable height.

Passing the Peace

Whether it is a handshake, a double handshake (both hands) or a hug, here is an opportunity for the congregation to move in a spontaneous and natural way. This gesture of warmth and sincere good will _is_ what it conveys. It is not just a sign of something that could or should be. It is, in itself, an action of Christian friendship and care for each person. If it is used each week, it may need a fresh introduction now and then, to keep it from becoming an empty formality. In many churches the people try to greet all the people around them and even move across aisles. Touch and eye contact are important elements of this greeting. A few minutes to internalize the meaning is often helpful in introducing the gesture.

Recall Christ's invitation to:

> love one another
> be reconciled to one another
> feed one another.

The PASSING OF THE PEACE might sometimes serve as an opening greeting. It should be used wherever it seems most natural and most meaningful. It can easily take on the central mood of a liturgy.

Swaying

Moving in harmony with the rhythm of the music or prayers is a way of internalizing the thought and feeling. In some Jewish communities, the Psalms are chanted accompanied by swaying. They refer to it as the "heart strings being tugged."

Clapping

Clapping is part of the movement that gives voice to the rhythms that we feel. Clapping should not replace singing, but add a pulsing drive to it. (For further discussion of CLAPPING, see THE CREATIVE MUSICIAN IN THE CHURCH, pp. 191-197)

APPLAUSE is sometimes a very natural way for people to give praise to God, yet there is a hesitation in many churches to do this. We need to reclaim this mode of expression, which has been lost to a misguided understanding of reverence. APPLAUSE for an uplifting choir or instrumental selection or a solo prayer-song shows appreciation to God for the gifts He has given to individuals and to the community, as well as gratitude to the persons themselves.

Shalom

"Shalom" is a beautiful Hebrew word that means "May you receive the fullness of God's peace and blessing. May you be all that God wants you to be." There is a Jewish custom of sharing "Shalom" with each person present at a family gathering. Two couples stand with right hands raised, touch palms and look into each other's eyes as they sing the entire verse. The couples separate and move on to find new partners to "Shalom." The singing and gestures continue until everyone has been included. This is a very special kind of blessing which can be used at the end of a camp or weekend experience, or other kinds of small group gatherings. I use the regular "Shalom" melody with the following words:

> Shalom, my friend, Shalom, my friend,
>
> Shalom, Shalom.
>
> May Christ be with you, may Christ be with you.
>
> Shalom, Shalom.

The Pacific Lutheran Liturgical Ensemble leads a congregational Doxology
at the Minneapolis Conference on Worship and the Arts. The first movement
consists of arms raised in a circle and then released on the word "flow."

The Doxology

Clap hands and carry the momentum up and around in an expanding circle of praise that flows into the next movement.

Praise God from whom all blessings flow.

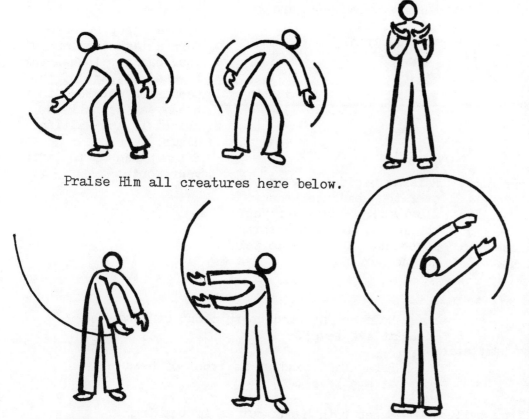

Gather the gifts, the creatures that are a part of your living. Hold them up in your hands as an offering.

Praise Him all creatures here below.

Encircle the universe, the <u>all</u> of life, to praise God.

Praise Him above, ye heavenly hosts.

Repeat the first movement. Use whatever gesture seems right for you to express the AMEN.

Praise Father, Son and Holy Ghost!   AMEN.

The Lord's Prayer

Our Father,
who is in heaven,

Raise arms upward in
an arc - dovetailing
with the arms of those
on either side - an
expression of "OUR"
Father.

holy is your name.

Bow head. Bring arms
with palms facing in,
toward your head and
bow low.

Your kingdom come.——— Right hand sweeps boldly
outward across body and
upward, palms up.

Your will be done _____

Left hand sweeps boldly
outward across body and
upward, palms up.

on earth as it is in heaven.

Turn hands palms down and
spread them out as if to
sense the earth.

With a scooping movement
form a basket or cup with
your hands. (When this
is used as part of the
Communion service, the
bread can actually be
placed in the waiting
hands.)
Bring hands up to touch
your mouth.

Give us this day
  our daily bread ————————————————

forgive us for our sins,

as we forgive those
who sin against us.

Raising hands a few inches
over the head, let them
slowly flow down over your
shoulders, as in a washing
movement. Turn and do this
to another person.

Bring right hand up in front of head
at eye level.

Lead us not into temptation

Bring left hand up in front of head
at eye level.

but deliver us from evil,——— Sweep both hands out as if pushing
the evil away.

for yours is the kingdom,
the power
and the glory forever.

Take hold of the hand of the person
on either side of you and raise the
hands a step higher on the words,
"power"..."glory"..."forever".

Amen.

Bend over, still holding hands and
then move upward in an energetic,
sweeping thrust.

The Use of Folk Dances

Folk dances, like folk songs, have grown from the experiences and needs of ordinary people. Through the ages, they have been an outlet for personal exuberance and communal celebration. Folk dancing has been a medium of socializing for young and old. It is, of course, much simpler to introduce folk dance in the liturgy if the people have some background and knowledge in this area, but this is very seldom the case. By introducing a simple circle dance to a group of people sharing in a religious service, you may be adding a new dimension to their understanding of community.

There are many folk dances that are suitable for use in religious celebration. Some are more appropriate for camp or retreat weekends, others can be woven into the closing of a liturgy. Some of the better known ones are: The Hora, Ma Navu, Mayim, Hineh Ma Tov, the Peace Prayer from Isaiah (printed on the next page). Circle and line dances seem to be more appropriate than set or partner dances. African and American Indian dances can be utilized as well as dances from the Balkans and the Middle East. Once you begin looking for possible congregational dances, you will probably draw from many sources. The things to keep in mind are:

> The steps should be uncomplicated so that newcomers
> can learn easily and join in.

> The music and words should express the spirit of the
> liturgical setting.

The CLOSING or SCATTERING is the most suitable place for such a dance. The circle (or circles) can be formed around the altar or around the church. Lines can move down the aisles and around the church, or right out of the doors and into the street.

There are occasions when a familiar circle dance can be adapted to express a portion of a Psalm or a simple phrase from the reading or the community prayer. New circle dances can be invented to move-out a Closing Hymn.

A joyous experience in sensing the oneness of a group that is moving together can do very much to build unity and hope in people. People need to HOPE together.

Peace Prayer

The following chant-dance is based upon Isaiah 2:4 which speaks of an everlasting peace and that people shall hammer their swords into plowshares, their spears into sickles and war shall not be taught.

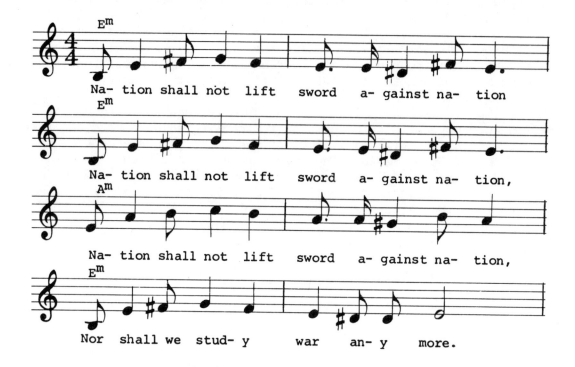

This dance incorporates the regular GRAPEVINE step, moving to the left. There is a flex, or bending of the knees on the first count. This bending gives a pulsing to the dance and makes it easy for people to join in. The movements and the song start slowly and then speed up as the dance progresses. Hands are extended along the adjoining person's arms, gripping wrists or elbows; or the hands may be extended across to opposite shoulders.

Nation shall not	Cross RIGHT FOOT behind LEFT FOOT and bend knees Step sideward on LEFT FOOT
lift sword	Cross RIGHT FOOT in front of LEFT FOOT
against nation	Step sideward on LEFT FOOT
Nation shall not	Cross RIGHT FOOT behind LEFT FOOT and bend knees Step sideward on LEFT FOOT
lift sword	Cross RIGHT FOOT in front of LEFT FOOT
against nation	Step sideward on LEFT FOOT

Continue the pattern throughout the rest of the dance

The PEACE DANCE may be done in a circle, in concentric circles or in a line. For an ending, the leader may free the left hand and draw the circle into a spiral. A final prayer or benediction within the tightly knit group is very effective.

Rise Up in the Mornin'

Sr. Adelaide Ortegel, S. P.

Al - le - lu — ia — Al - le-lu — ia —

There's a Spir - it in — the air. — Feel it mov - in'

ev' — ry-where — call - in' us — to jump- a -board — and

rise up in the morn-in' in the joy of the Lord . —

Al - le - lu — ia — Al - le -lu — ia —

From the hymnal, COME SHARE THE SPIRIT.
Copyright © 1975, The Center For Contemporary Celebration.

A Possible Circle Dance for RISE UP IN THE MORNIN'

Alleluia - Alleluia
Alleluia - Alleluia

Sideward step RIGHT foot, close; sideward step LEFT foot, close. Flex knee on 4th count. This step is repeated with each of the "Alleluias."

There's a spirit in the air

Cross RIGHT foot over LEFT, step sideward on LEFT, cross RIGHT foot behind LEFT, step sideward on LEFT.

Feel it movin' everywhere

Cross LEFT foot over RIGHT, step sideward on RIGHT, cross LEFT foot behind RIGHT, step sideward on RIGHT.

Callin' us to jump aboard

Everyone turn toward center of circle and take small steps in. Clasped hands reach up and touch on the last beat of "aboard."

And rise up in the mornin'
in the joy of the Lord!

Still holding hands, the circle is opened, each person moving back as far as stretched arms will permit. On the word "joy" the circle is pulled back into the beginning position.

131

Folk Dancing a Familiar Hymn

The hymn, "They'll Know We Are Christians" by Peter Scholtes, is a favorite one, sung around the world. The circle dance which appears in the right column is an easy step to do while singing this song. It should be done at a moderate tempo.

Form circle - facing in.
All clap on the beat.

Join hands and turn sharply to the RIGHT.
Take 3 steps to the RIGHT on the beat.

Turn sharply to the LEFT and take 3 steps to the LEFT on the beat.

With hands still joined take small steps into the center of the circle.

Raise joined hands slowly to highest reach.
Let them burst open on the word "restored."

As the chorus is sung:

Let arms sweep around to shoulders of person on either side of you, and begin swaying to the right, then left, and so on.

This dance design is especially good for small group meetings, the closing of a conference or a weekend experience where people have shared much of themselves. The words are usually known by most of the group. All four stanzas can be done the same way.

Sufi Dances of Universal Peace

A chapter on communal religious dancing would not be complete without some mention of the American Sufi Dancing. The Dances of Universal Peace are a collection of group-dances set to sacred phrases from the various world religions.

It was in 1968 and 1969 that Murshid Samuel Lewis, leader of the San Francisco Sufi disciples, began developing the devotional dances. The first few were simple follow-the-leader type dances or walks which used either "Allah, Allah," or "Om Sri Ram Jai Ram Jai Jai Ram," the divine Name of God which stands at the center of all the dances like a pulse-beat. The chanting of the sacred phrase was the foundation of the movement. Gradually, other forms were added, mostly drawn from world folk-dances. Murshid had done much folk dancing in his youth. As he watched his disciples find spiritual joy and growth in the dances, his vision began to grow. He visited Ruth St. Denis and shared with her his dream to bring about world peace through dancing. He was both encouraged and inspired by her.

His dances include several Shaker songs, A Christian Resurrection dance and a Jewish Shalom blessing, as well as a rich variety of Muslim and Hindu dance chants.

> "Peace will come to the Middle East," said Murshid Lewis, "when Muslims, Christians and Jews eat together, dance together and pray together to the glory of the one God."

Since his death in 1971, the repertoire of Spiritual Dances continues to expand. His followers have refined and co-ordinated the dance movements and the singing of God's Names. A good recording is available. There are a number of centers throughout this country where seekers may experience this type of religious dancing.

> "The Dance is the way of life; the Dance is the sway of life. What life gives may be expressed with body, heart and soul to the glory of God and the elevation of mankind, leading therein to ecstasy and self-realization. VERILY, THIS IS THE SACRED DANCE.
>
> When doctrines divide and 'isms' turn man against man, without speech, without silence, let us demonstrate. Let these demonstrations manifest everywhere. Not what we think or say, BUT WHAT WE DO SHALL AVAIL. May we therefore bear the torch of holiness and make of our bodies temples of sacred worship. Verily, man is the noblest work of God."

Murshid Samuel Lewis
(from <u>Spiritual Dancing</u>,
an unpublished manuscript.)

Universal Peace Dance Mantras

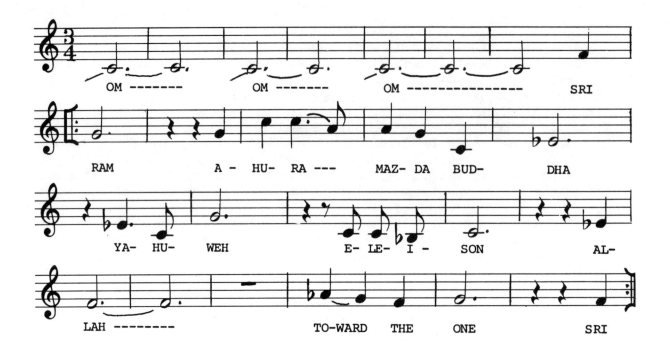

OM ------- OM ------- OM --------------- SRI

RAM A - HU - RA --- MAZ- DA BUD- DHA

YA- HU- WEH E- LE- I - SON AL-

LAH -------- TO-WARD THE ONE SRI

SRI RAM: Deep bow to the center of the circle with hands in prayerful position over the heart. (All turn and face counterclockwise.)

AHURA MAZDA: Hands held above the head in sun position.

BUDDHA: Hands in prayerful position first touching forehead, lips and then the heart in slight bow.

YA HUVWEH (YAHWEH): Hands are extended in front of one, palms open, slightly raised.

ELEISON: Hands and arms are raised up and spread out.

ALLAH: All spin.

TOWARD THE ONE: All hands extended in front facing the center of the circle.

This dance may be done as many times as the leader designates. At the end all join hands and say OM OM OM.

FURTHER READING

Adams, Doug. Congregational Dancing in Christian Worship. Revised edition,
    1975. The Sharing Company, P.O. Box 190, North Aurora, IL 60542.

Delakova, Katya & Fred Berk. Jewish Folk Dance Book. 1948. 45pp. Order
    from The Dance Mart, Box 48, Homecrest Station, Brooklyn, New York 11229.

Eshkol-Wachmann Movement Notation:
    Folk Dances of Israel: The Yemenite Dance, 1972. 130pp.
    Folk Dances of Israel: Dances from the Yemen and Israeli Folk Dances.
        1970. 101pp.
        Order from The Dance Mart, Box 48, Homecrest Station, Brooklyn, NY 11229.

Mynatt, Constance V. and Bernard D. Kaiman. Folk Dancing for Students and
    Teachers. Wm. C. Brown Company Publishers, 1968. Dubuque, Iowa.

Sufi Dance and Walk

Dances of Universal Peace, Vol. I and Vol. II. from the works of Murshid
    Samuel L. Lewis. Sufi Islamia Ruhaniat Society.

The Sufi Dance and Song Record.
    This material may be ordered from The Rainbow Bridge, P.O. Box 40208,
    San Francisco, CA 94120.

let's have a

WORKSHOP

Planning the Workshop

A time of creating in dance and movement is always a "workshop" activity. Some workshops are planned to be one-time events and then develop into on-going sessions. Bonds of friendship and lasting spirit often grow from these times of sharing.

A workshop in dance can take many forms and fulfill a wide variety of needs. The mutual interchange of ideas and involvement in creative expression can

- add a new dimension to the religious education program,

- be an extension of a youth program,

- be the starting point for drawing together the nucleus of a dance choir,

- help more people to grow in an experiential understanding of dance and creative movement,

- provide an interest in dance as therapy,

- afford dance groups with the opportunity to share and expand new ideas and thereby gather fresh impetus and inspiration.

As you begin planning a dance workshop, give careful consideration to the PURPOSE and to the FOCUS of the event. For WHOM are you designing the workshop? It will be important for you to define this clearly in your publicity communications. You have to bring something to a workshop in order to take something away. People need to know what will be offered and what will be expected. Too often, the emphasis is a general 'just get the people to come and let things happen.' This usually results in a frustrating experience for both leader and participants.

Start with a CORE GROUP

You will need to gather a dedicated CORE GROUP to get the planning session underway. It will take teamwork to organize and publicize the workshop. An enthusiastic CORE GROUP can overcome difficulties and provide valuable personal contacts. No matter how well an event is publicized in papers and bulletins, no matter how many flyers you send out, the strongest drawing card to a workshop is personal contact. Dance is still such a specialized area that most people will be somewhat hesitant to risk themselves. They need that extra touch of assurance that a personal invitation can give.

The Planning Session

At your first planning session, which should take place well in advance of the event, you will need to give careful consideration to the following:

WHO WILL IT BE FOR? WHO IS LIKELY TO ATTEND?

WHAT WILL THE FOCUS BE?

WHO WILL THE LEADERS BE?

WHEN? Be sure to check the calendar for any scheduling
       conflicts.

WHERE? Check the space requirements and the location of
       the building. Is it easily accessible?

TIME SCHEDULE? Is this a day workshop or longer?

EQUIPMENT NEEDS?

WHAT IS THIS GOING TO COST? Include the honorariums for
       leadership, refreshments, materials, publicity,
       mailings and rentals.

REGISTRATION? Set a deadline for registrations. Decide
       where they will be sent and how much the fees will
       be? Designate one person to take care of registration
       on the day of the workshop.

Publicity

When the above questions have been answered, you are ready to begin work on publicizing the event and contacting people personally. You should check into what mailings are available to you through local churches and art agencies. You should plan to write news releases for local papers and to accompany these with photos of dancers in action. Contact the local radio and television media for public announcements.

Often the DANCE WORKSHOP is tucked into an Arts Festival Weekend or a yearly conference. Sometimes the WORKSHOP is sandwiched in as an optional event among many others. In this case, the participants may come with a wide spectrum of needs and expectations. The planning, in such cases, becomes more difficult because the leaders bear the burden of being all things to all people. When you are in this situation, it is usually better to plan the session and publicize the event in the line of a Creative Movement and Improvisation session, with time for questions and discussion. If trained dancers attend, the sensitive leader can find ways to keep them on the creating edge and still meet the more basic needs of those who have never danced before.

Hopes for Growth

After the initial planning stage, the next step is to look at the design of the workshop for qualities that will bring about the kind of growth the people will need.

TECHNICAL GROWTH - will there be a chance for participants to stretch beyond their present ability and style of moving? Will there be live performance, artistic enrichment and films of quality?

SPIRITUAL GROWTH - Will the person's spiritual dimension have a chance to expand? Will there be an opportunity for shared religious celebration?

COMMUNAL GROWTH - Will there be time for spontaneous sharing of ideas and visions? Will the tone of the workshop build toward wholeness and a sense of one-ness in Body?

CREATIVE GROWTH - Will the person be challenged to use imaginative and improvisational skills? Will there be an opportunity to develop an idea and express it to the whole group?

All of these aspects of growth overlap and augment each other. It is far better to evaluate your program using some of these questions BEFORE the workshop happens rather than AFTER the event. A written evaluation form at the close of a stimulating experience is a contradiction to the concept of communication through experiential movement. If you want feed-back on your teaching, build it into the workshop format. Hopefully, your leaders will be skilled, sensitive artists who can sense how the people are reacting as the workshop is in progress.

The FOCUS and GROWTH areas should be shared with all the leaders ahead of time. They will then be able to set common goals for their own particular sessions. The leaders will know by the feeling tones and enthusiasm (or lack of it), just how the workshop sessions went. The planning group and leaders may want to get together and evaluate the over-all development and outcome of the day in order to plan for future workshop experiences.

The Opening

The way you welcome the people will set a tone for the time ahead. Here is the place for the CORE GROUP to use its collective skills in hospitality and organization. Preparation will need to be made for swift registration of names, addresses and phone numbers. Coffee, tea or soft drinks should be available for early arrivers. Set up resource tables for viewing.

If you are planning for a large group, prepare some total group experience at the beginning before folks are sent off to separate sessions. Plan for total group events throughout the day. Your sense of pacing and awareness of human needs will guide your structuring.

Possible Schedules

An Evening and A Day Workshop

    Session One
        Friday 7:30 p.m. to 10 p.m.
            Registration
            Warm-ups, creative movement sequence closing
               with dance in a fluid light environment.

    Session Two
        Saturday 9:00 a.m. to 12:00 p.m.
            Warm-ups and techniques with further creatings
               in pairs and in groups.

      Lunch

    Session Three
        Saturday 1:00 p.m. to 2:00 p.m.
            Film and discussion.

          2:30 p.m. to 4:00 p.m.
          Compositional work, sharing personal expressions,
          workshop creations and a celebration which brings
          the day to a meaningful close.

A Day Workshop

    Session One
        9:30 a.m.
            Registration
            Warm-ups, creative movement and group improvisation.
        12:00 p.m.
            Lunch

    Session Two
        1:00 p.m.
            Designing Dance Statements
        3:00 p.m.
            Sharing the creating and a closing celebration event
            appropriate for the day.

Be sure to provide time for discussion. People usually want help in the
following areas:

        How do you get a dance group started?

        How do you introduce the idea of dance into the local church?

        What should a dance group wear?

        Is taped or live music better?

There are no final answers to these questions. Most often, people will have to rely on their own judgement and artistic sensitivity in the particular situation. The value of such discussion is that it opens the minds of the people to the fact that there are many possibilities, alternatives and approaches to every situation.

Space for Dance

A large room with open space is the first necessity. The floor should be clear and clean, since the dancers usually work with bare feet. A carpeted room can be used for some of the awareness exercises, but wood or tile floors are necessary for dancing and most of the other exercises. It is useful to have some rooms available for small group work. You will also need a place for changing clothes.

If the focus of the workshop is on liturgical dance, then some of the experiences should take place in a worship setting. If the focus is on creative movement and growth in awareness, consider the possibility of an outdoor session.

It is a good idea to change the environment for the second session. If you can't change rooms, change the lighting. Use overhead projectors and some colored transparencies. Refer to LIGHT: A LANGUAGE OF CELEBRATION for fluid light effects. A fresh environment will awaken the imagination and prepare people for new explorations.

Use of Films

There are many films on a variety of dance styles. A listing is offered on page 145 of this book. The time after lunch or after supper is a good opportunity for film viewing and discussion. Choose films that will supplement the activities of the workshop. Preview the films so that you will be prepared to answers questions.

Dance and Music

While much of the work in creative movement and improvisation will be done without music, you will want to be able to offer resources in this area. Plan for a table of recordings, tapes, sheet music and books for browsing. Sometimes it is possible to invite people to bring resources which they have found valuable and to display these on a resource table. Write to music publishers for additional display materials. Also, your Public Library may have an assortment of records and tapes that could be used.

Kent Schneider's Book THE CREATIVE MUSICIAN IN THE CHURCH has an interesting section on the experience of a dancer writing her own song to be sung and danced (see pages 135-138). Some of the musical resources listed on pp. 144 to 147 of this book, A DANCING PEOPLE, will provide new listening and dance resources. By adding some music to the third session of the workshop, you will be creating another type of environment.

Meals

If lunch or supper is provided, it should be a light meal. A practical suggestion is to ask the people to bring a sack lunch or finger food for sharing. The host can provide beverages. The shared meal becomes a surprising smorgasbord. Be sure to list the instructions to bring a sack lunch in the publicity material.

Closings

The workshop event should close with some kind of a gathering that will send people off with a feeling of connection and encouragement. If there is a dance choir or individual artist available, a live performance can beautifully re-inforce the learnings and insights of the day. The closing should be a festive event and a prayerful 'Amen' to the day. Don't make it too complicated. Let it be a natural flow of the day. Remember that the people will be tired. They have gained many new ideas and insights. The closing should be an insightful drawing together of the meanings that have been shared.

The Sacred Dance Guild

An excellent on-going resource is the membership and newsletter offered by the Sacred Dance Guild of America. This non-profit organization, with a growing membership, was created by dancers and dance leaders to promote dance as a religious expression. The newsletter contains announcements of Dance Workshops and Institutes, Film and Book Reviews, and descriptions of sacred dance events which are designed by members all over the country. A membership listing makes it possible to contact dance leaders in your own area. For membership information write:

Mrs. John Alderdice
124 Fenway
Rockville Center, N.Y. 11570

The Guild also publishes some helpful booklets for designing workshops. Contact the Helps and Guidelines Director:

Mrs. Frederic Volz
24 Tyler Rd.
Lexington, MA 02173

Resources on Record

There is such a variety of possibilities for using recorded music with dance that I can only mention a few of the recordings that I've found basic for any dancing library. The following recommendations list the album title, the artist, label number and those songs that I've found useful.

Jazz

CELEBRATION FOR MODERN MAN by Kent Schneider, band and voices. Available through the Center.

Soundings For New Beginnings, Psalm 150, A Mighty Fortress, Church Within Us.

SILVER CYCLES by Eddie Harris Atlantic SD 1517.

Silver Cycles, Electric Ballad. Features sax and echoplex effects.

SECOND MOVEMENT by Eddie Harris & Les McCann. Atlantic SD 1583.

Set Us Free (10:28) is a rhythmicly freeing sound for workshop or worship service.

SONRISE jazz-rock by Kent Schneider, band and voices. Available through The Center.

Travelin' 40 Days is composed for dancers, multimedia projection and band. Woodlawn Walk is 7/4 blues.

A LOVE SUPREME by John Coltrane. Impulse A-77.

A spiritual offering by avante garde genuis. Deep.

BAROQUE SKETCHES by Art Farmer. Columbia CS 9388

Jesu, Rhythm of Life (from "Sweet Charity") are two fine instrumental works for spirited movement.

OUTSTANDING JAZZ COMPOSITIONS OF THE 20th CENTURY. Columbia C2L31.

A two record set of great sounds, particularly, Revelations.

BRASS ROOTS by Doc Severinsen. RCA 4522.

Psalm 150 is a powerhouse sound for the dance group. Also exciting for workshop improvisation.

JAZZ SUITE ON THE MASS TEXTS by Paul Horn. RCA 3414.

Follows the Latin Mass, arranged for voices and large orchestra. Has many useful tracks and is very useable in the liturgical setting.

A NEW PERSPECTIVE by Donald Byrd with band and voices. Blue Note 4124.

Cristo Redentor, Elijah, Chant, Beast of Burden and The Black Disciple.

THE CHUCK MANGIONE QUARTET by Chuck Mangione. Mercury 1-631.

Land of Make Believe, Floating, Little Sunflower.

ALL THE CHILDREN CRIED by John Klemmer. Cadet LPS 326.

All The Children Cried, Journey's End, Here Comes The Child, I Whisper A Prayer For Peace.

The Music of Meditation

SILVER APPLES OF THE MOON
by Morton Subotnick

This is music that floats and dives, feels and crashes. Very good for improvisation.

HOLY MUSIC by Malachi
Verve V6-5024

Spontaneous music for meditative moods.

JOURNEY IN SATCHIDANANDA by
Alice Coltrane. Impulse AS 9203.

Satchidananda means wisdom. The record combines jazz and Indian moods.

COSMIC CONSCIOUSNESS by Paul
Horn. World Pacific WPS
21445

Music of meditation with flute and Indian instrumentation.

Films on Dance

ACROBATS OF GOD. 22 min. 1969, color. May be rented from the U. of Ill. or from Pyramid. It is a filming of Martha Graham's comic vision of the creative process.

AIR FOR THE G-STRING. 7 min. Doris Humphrey and a group of four in a beautifully filmed version of her early dance work, choreographed in 1928. Available from Dance Films.

DANCE: FOUR PIONEERS (Martha Graham, Doris Humphrey, Charles Weidman, Hanya Holm), National Educational Television. 29 min. 1965. May be rented from U. of Ill. or Indiana U.

A DANCER'S WORLD. 30 min. 1957. One of the most beautiful dance films ever made. As she dresses for the role of Jocasta, Martha Graham discusses the life, the art, and the craft of the dancer. Her dancers, in the studio, flow through dance patterns from the Graham vocabulary and repertory. Available from many Public Libraries. McGraw-Hill Text-Film Division, New York.

MIME OF MARCEL MARCEAU. 23 min. color, 1972. May be rented from the U. of Illinois. Sequences show performance and rehearsals. May be purchased from Learning Corporation of America, 711 Fifth Ave. NY 10022.

PROCESSION: CONTEMPORARY DIRECTIONS IN AMERICAN DANCE, University of California Extension Media Center, Berkeley, CA.

TOTEM (ALWIN NIKOLAIS), 16 min. color, 1963. A film interpretation by Ed Emshwiller of a dance work by Nikolais. Grove Press Film Division, New York.

For further films and discussion notes see:

FILMS ON BALLET & MODERN DANCE: NOTES AND A DIRECTORY
by John Mueller

American Dance Guild
245 West 52nd Street
New York, NY 10019

Music for Movement

The following arrangements and compositions are designed to be choreographed. They provide opportunities for improvisation, both by the musicians and the dancers. These are some of the musical resources available from The Center. Write for a free catalog of the Celebration Music Series.

MIGHTY FORTRESS arr. by Kent Schneider for organ, congregation, SATB choir, jazz ensemble of trumpet, tenor and alto saxes, piano, bass and drums. As recorded on the album CELEBRATION FOR MODERN MAN. $8.00

PRAISE YE THE LORD arr. by Schneider for SATB choir, congregation, jazz ensemble of trumpet, tenor sax, piano, bass and drums. The familiar hymn is set to an energetic jazz waltz tempo, building to a final shout of "Praise." $4.00

BREAD OF PRESENCE by Schneider is a rocking, gospel hymn which affirms that wherever bread is shared there are no strangers. This communion song is arranged for SATB choir, trumpet, tenor and alto saxes, trombone, piano, bass and drums. Recorded on SONRISE album. $5.00

LORD, INSPIRE OUR WORSHIP by Schneider is an opening hymn for congregation, unison choir, trumpet, tenor and alto saxes, piano bass and drums. Jazz improvisational-style $6.00

ALL THAT HAS LIFE, PRAISE GOD! by Schneider is a setting of Psalm 150 for SATB choir, trumpet, tenor and alto saxes, piano, bass, drums and organ. Recorded on CELEBRATION FOR MODERN MAN album. Includes Conductor's Guide. $8.00

CREATE IN ME by Schneider is a meditative setting of Psalm 51, arranged for voice, trumpet, tenor and alto saxes, piano, bass, drums and percussion. The slow tempo of this work allows for much dance interpretation. $5.00

SOUNDINGS FOR NEW BEGINNINGS by Schneider is a bossa nova prelude with opportunities for extended improvisation by horns and dancers. Arranged for trumpet, tenor and alto saxes, piano, bass, drums and scat choir with Conductor's Guide. Recorded on CELEBRATION FOR MODERN MAN. $8.00

LOVERS-ARE SPECIAL PEOPLE by Schneider is a meditation in 3/4 and bossa nova for a trio of flutes, piano, bass and drums. A nice, light work with extended solos. $2.00

THE FAITHFUL GATHER by Schneider is a subtle, rocking instrumental for gathering the people. Arranged for trumpet, tenor sax, piano, bass and drums. $4.00

WOODLAWN WALK by Schneider is a 7/4 blues tune arranged for trumpet, flute, tenor sax and trombone, or any combination of two horns, with piano, bass and drums. A joyously refreshing journey to dance out. Recorded on SONRISE records. $3.00

AMAZING GRACE arr. by Jim McBride is an exciting setting of this folk favorite. An instrumental setting precedes the communal singing. A flexible arrangement for choir, alto and tenor saxes, trumpet, piano, bass and drums. New words by Sr. Adelaide. $6.00

WE THREE KINGS arr. by Schneider brings an up-tempo setting of this Christmas carol. Arranged for trumpet, soprano sax or tenor sax, piano, bass and drums. $4.00

GREET A NEW DAY by Schneider is a great sound for the morning. A 3/4 jazz waltz at a moderate tempo is arranged for trumpet, tenor sax, scat voice or flute, piano, bass and drums. Ample improvisation. $3.00

TRAVELIN' 40 DAYS by Schneider is an extended work using styles of jazz, rock, slow ballad and chorale. Composed for dancers, multimedia projection. Includes Conductor's Guide, SATB choir, solo voices, trumpet, tenor and alto sax, trombone, piano, guitar, bass and drums. Recorded on SONRISE records. This is an exciting choir and dance concert piece. $9.00

Marylu Milano dances to the dramatic TRAVELIN' 40 DAYS, accompanied by musicians and media projections in The Sonrise of Imagination concert of new religious music, Chicago, 1973.

INDEX

Alleluia 31,122
Amen 31,122
American Indians 8
Anderson Dance Group 109,36
Applause 125
Artist 22,23,43
Awareness 18-23, 108
Beckman, Kathy Iverson 49-61, pic.48,50
Body of Christ 83-85, 87-90
Breathing 4,28,29,94
Calvin, John 14,86
Carols 13
Celebration 38,40,45,51-53
Centering 25-27,94
Charting the Liturgy 92-93
Congregational Movement 118-120,126-132
                         Sufi 134

Children 24,116
Christ Takes Form 118
Clapping 125
Clic 73,75
Class Design 109-115
Clown 71,72
Communication 44,64,84
Communion 44,83-86,99-100
Confession 98-99
Cosmic Breathing 28-29
Creation's Story 95-96
Creativity 22-23,90
Dance Experiences 33,90,130,132,134
Doxology 126-127
Duncan, Isadora 15
Early Christians 10,85
Earth Song, script 93-104
Electronic Music 8,145
Energy 57
Errett, Gayda 46, pic. 38,45
Exercises & Explorations 25-31,73-75,
                          110-116

Faith 40,45-46
Feldenkrais, Dr. Moshe 18-19
Film 142,145
Fluid Light Environments 117,141-142
Folk Dancing 13,129-132, Sufi 133-135
Gesture 31,64,69,76
Getting Beneath the Surface, script 78-80
Graham, Martha 15
Greek 8,10,12
Greeting 94
Gregory the Great 13
Hands 124
Hebrew 9,10
Historical Background 4-12,83-87
Hyams-Burton, L'Ana 40-42
Hymn of Jesus 11
Hymn-sandwich 87
Improvisation 90
In the Beginning, poem 3-8
Isaiah, Peace Prayer Dance 130
Jazz 15,87,144
Kamin, Dan 78-80

Knox, John 86
Leadership 120-121
Lewis, Murshid Samuel 133-135
Life Is a Circle, music 102-104, dance 101
Light, projected 46,117,142
Liturgy 14,24,51-53,59-60,76-79,81-105
Liturgical Dance Ensemble, Pacific Lutheran
    University pic. 48,50,54,59
Lord's Prayer 128
Manuscript Culture 87-90
Marceau, Marcel 62-69
Mass with Dance 46-47
Meditation 25-27,94,97
Mime 63-80
Milano, Marylu 8, pic. 34,147
Ministry of Dance 42-43
Movement Prayers 31,121
Multi-media 45,142
Music Resources 94-96,99,144-147
Offering 126-127, Doxology 89,99
Passing the Peace 124-125
Peace Prayer, Isaiah 130
Processions 123-124
Profane 86
Publicity 139
Reformation 14,86
Religious Dance 5-15,39
Responding Relationships 113-115
Rise Up in the Mornin' 131
Roman 8-9,12
Sacred 39-41,86
Sacred Dance Guild 143
Schneider, Rev. Kent 82, 83-105, 142
Scripts,
         Earth Song 93-104
Sensory Awareness 18
Shalom 125
Sharing 113-115
Shawn, Ted 17
Shiva 2
Sorell, Walter 9
Space 142
Spatial design 56
Spirit-Bodied 5,83-85
St. Augustine 13
St. Basil 85
St. Denis, Ruth 15
Standing 122
Sufi Dances 133-135
Swaying 125
Symbols 89,91
Tau Cross 122
They'll Know We Are Christians 132
Time 57
Tribal Culture 4-7,32
Universal Peace Dance Mantras, Sufi 134
Warm-ups 110
Wholeness 17-19,24-35,88,108
Workshops 21,36,45,138-142
Yoga 25,28-29